Positioning
for Professionals

Positioning for Professionals

*How Professional Knowledge
Firms Can Differentiate
Their Way to Success*

Tim Williams

WILEY

John Wiley & Sons, Inc.

Published by John Wiley & Sons, Inc., Hoboken, New Jersey.

Published simultaneously in Canada.

Library of Congress Cataloging-in-Publication Data:

Williams, Tim, 1954—
    Positioning for professionals : how professional knowledge firms can differentiate their way to success / Tim Williams.
       p.   cm.
    Includes index.
    ISBN 978-0-470-58715-7 (hardback); 978-0-470-87735-7 (ebk); 978-0-470-87751-7 (ebk); 978-0-470-87752-4 (ebk)
    1. Branding (Marketing)   2. Success in business.   I. Title.
    HF5415.1255.W55   2010
    658.8'27—dc22

                                                                    2010021337

Printed in the United States of America
10 9 8 7 6 5 4 3 2 1

To my wife and lifetime companion, Christine

Contents

Chapter 8
Without Execution, There Is No Strategy

83

Chapter 9
Getting Paid for Creating Value

121

Chapter 10
A New and Better Way to Price
Professional Services

133

Quick, which airline do you associate with the following?

"We invite you to sit back, relax, and enjoy your flight with us today. If there's anything we can do to make your flight more enjoyable, please just let us know."

Your answer is probably "every airline." That's because pretty much every airline uses the same language on every flight. There is, of course, the government-mandated safety language that every airline must include in its on-board announcements; but beyond that there is a missed opportunity for airlines to say something *different*. There's also an opportunity for airlines to *do* something different, but most don't. The result is that you don't know whether you're flying Delta, United, or American. And chances are you don't care.

The airlines are just doing what most other companies do: copying their competitors. In a business context, imitation is not "the most sincere form of flattery"; it's just lazy. When you really think about it, copying someone else's business model demonstrates an incredible lack creativity and imagination. Yet most business and brands are just copies of someone else's.

Most managers invest their time and energy in trying to make their brands better, when in fact they should be working to make their brands *different*. Better isn't necessarily always better; different is better. Behind the scenes, American Airlines may be working hard to recruit the best people, deliver the most efficient service, and build the best maintenance record. But most of that means very little to customers unless their experience with American is actually different than with other airlines.

NO SUCH THING AS A COMMODITY

One definition of a brand is that consumers are willing to spend more money for it than for a similar "product" in the category. Airlines no doubt feel that they are in a constant price war with their competitors. Their explanation will be that airline travel is viewed as a commodity, and that their customers "just want to get from point A to point B at the lowest price." The problem is that there is really no such thing as a commodity.

Organizations like airlines feel that they are a special case, that other categories are much easier to "brand" than theirs. Their defense is that a brand like Starbucks has a real advantage since it's obviously easier to develop strong brand affinity for a coffee house than an airline. Really? Why then were there no strong coffee house brands until Starbucks came along? Starbucks built a reputation selling a product that's over 90 percent water. That's because they understand that they're not just selling a product, but the experience of the product.

Actually water itself is another startling example of the power of branding. Covering over 75 percent of the earth's surface, it could be argued that water is the *ultimate* commodity. Nothing is so widely used and distributed as water. Yet millions of people are willing to pay up to *one thousand* times the cost tap water for one liter of it. That's because of water quality questions, you say? That doesn't explain the pricing disparity between various brands of bottled water on the supermarket shelf. In a blind taste test, could one really discern the difference between Crystal Geyser spring water (selling for 59 cents per liter) and Evian spring water (selling for 99 cents per liter—very close to double the price)? In restaurants, branded spring water can sell for up to $7.50 per liter.

If water can do it, why can't an airline? Or a hotel, or a steel company, or a law firm, or an advertising agency? They can. They just need to stop copying every hotel, steel company, law firm, or agency they compete with.

THE URGE TO COPY

The urge to copy is exceptionally strong in the human species. The underlying explanation is the "copying" mechanism that has allowed humans to survive and evolve for the past few millions years. The work of social observers like Mark Earls demonstrates the simple truth that humans are social creatures, not independent agents, and that as such they rely on copying to learn and survive in society. In fact, says Earls, "Copying is our species' number one learning and adaptive strategy."[1]

So building a successful brand means going against your instincts. Common sense would tell you to closely examine what competitors in the category are doing, make sure you are offering the same or better features, and adopt the "best practices" in the industry. But while others are studying and following best practices, the innovators and category leaders are developing the "next practices." They are resisting the natural urge to copy. And instead of just working to improve their brand, they are working to differentiate it.

THE BEST AND ALL THE REST

This explains the alarming disparity between the world's top brands and all the rest. Because most brands are more likely to copy than to innovate, the measurement referred to as "brand equity" has been in decline on average since 2004. But a handful of leading brands actually are growing in brand equity. In fact, what the consultancy Core Brand calls "brand equity value" is concentrated among the top 100 brands, which account for over 90 percent of all brand equity value.[2] This isn't because the top 100 brands outspend their competitors, but because they out-differentiate them.

The reason top brands in a category outpace their rivals is not the power of share of market (as regularly taught in business schools), but rather their share of mind. This is the power of the brand. While companies may occupy a position on the stock exchange, brands occupy a position in the mind of the customer. This is how the term "positioning" was coined. Positioning is the foundation of branding, because it identifies what the brand stands for.

ALIGNMENT IS EVERYTHING

Unless you know what the brand stands for, how can you possibly make effective decisions about how to run your business? Consider how a clearly defined positioning can lead you to good answers to critical questions like:

- What services and capabilities should we support and develop?
- Who are our best prospective customers and clients?
- How should the firm be structured?
- What should we be doing more of? Less of?
- What kind of business partnerships do we need?
- What kind of knowledge and expertise do we need to cultivate?
- How should the enterprise be structured?
- What type of people do we need to hire?
- What kind of training and professional development should we provide?
- What should our website say?
- What should our offices look like?

Every decision you make about your business either contributes to or detracts from your desired brand; very few are neutral. Business decisions can't be made in a vacuum or based on some vague notion of "excellence." The enterprises that make the best decisions are the ones with the clearest view of who they are and what makes them different. In other words, they are companies with a positioning.

POSITIONING IS NOT COMMON SENSE

Especially in tough economic times, "common sense" would suggest that a business can improve its revenue streams by expanding products and services, broadening capabilities, and appealing to more customers. It seems like common sense, but it's exactly the wrong response. The best growth strategy—in good economies or bad—is to decide what *not* to do. The best way to expand is by narrowing.

Imagine two architectural firms: one that's extremely focused with a clear value proposition, and one with an unfocused business strategy that attempts to do everything for everybody. Which of these two firms would have:

1. The greatest earning power?
2. The largest geographical market area?
3. The fewest competitors?
4. The greatest degree of respect from clients?
5. The most sophisticated clients?

The answer in every case is the focused firm. Let's look at each question individually.

Greater Earning Power

It's a simple fact that the specialist earns more than the generalist. This is true in medicine, law, engineering, architecture, consulting, construction—you name it. This is because the specialist knows more, and we live and work in a knowledge economy.

Larger Geographical Market Area

Focused firms draw clients from all over the globe, not just from their own zip code. That's because what they're selling isn't available down the block from some other firm just like them.

Fewer Competitors

The easiest way to narrow your competition is to narrow your focus. There are far fewer specialists than generalists, and the law of supply and demand dictates that the less the supply, the greater the demand.

More Respect from Clients

Knowledge and expertise equal respect. An effective value proposition allows your firm to develop and leverage its intellectual capital. This makes you valued—and respected—not just for what you do, but for what you know.

More Sophisticated Clients

A quality value proposition attracts a quality client. A business that proclaims, "We're right for everybody," logically is going to attract both the good and the bad.

The counterintuitive solution to business success is to narrow your focus, not expand it.

A BRAND DEVELOPMENT GUIDE FOR PROFESSIONAL FIRMS

Professional firms like advertising agencies, law firms, and accounting firms usually see themselves as counselors and advisors that work *for* brands rather than being brands themselves. Firms staffed with knowledge workers usually resist the concept of marketing (the ultimate irony: advertising agencies that don't advertise). But the truth is every company is a brand whether it wants to be or not. You can be a brand either by design or by default.

In professional services—as in packaged goods—customers buy brands, not products. As we'll discuss throughout this book, a brand is the customer's *idea* of the product. While a product or company exists in reality, a brand exists only in someone's head. But it's this perception of your firm that drives all customer behavior.

YOUR FIRM'S VALUE PROPOSITION

Defining your brand is synonymous with defining your value proposition. On the surface, this may feel like a soft concept until you examine what it really means. Quite simply, a "value proposition" is an articulation of the value you create for your clients. Ultimately, this is the most important strategic planning a business enterprise can engage in.

A strong value proposition means a strongly focused team, a strongly appealing business model, and ultimately a strong margin. More than one business consultant has observed, "No margin, no mission." The starting point for discussions of lofty concepts like mission and vision is *value*. A business exists to create value outside of itself. Indeed, creating value is the only reason for a commercial enterprise to exist in the first place.

A phrase like "value proposition" always begs the question, "What is value?" While value can be economic, rational, emotional, or even social, ultimately real value shows up on your client's bottom line. Your firm exists to create this value.

THE TRUTH OF YOUR BRAND

How do you go about defining your value proposition? Start by clearing your mind of shop-worn concepts like "quality," "leadership," and "delighting customers." It's not that they're not important; they've just lost their meaning. This kind of hyperbolic language also does nothing to distinguish your offering from others. And it does little to get you to the real question of value.

In truth, you have a value proposition whether you know it or not, and every value proposition will fall somewhere in the following three areas: points of parity, points of relevance, or points of difference. Each is explained here.

> **Points of Parity** are those that are generic to the category. Professional firms are expected to deliver excellent client service, quality work, and so on. When firms lean on points such as "full service," "wide range of experience," or "attention of senior people" as their value proposition, they are contributing to the vast sea of sameness in professional services.
>
> **Points of Relevance** are a step in the right direction. Simply asking the "relevance" question means you are narrowing your target from

"everybody" to "somebody." Rather than a generic listing of generic benefits, it is a specific listing of specific benefits based on relevance to a particular type of client or category.

Points of Difference are the highest order and point the way toward the defining and articulating your value proposition. They also are obviously the most difficult to define, because they involve the most sacrifice. By articulating a point of difference, you are saying not only what you are, but what you are not.

Not surprisingly, most value propositions fall squarely into the points of parity area because the leaders of the firm haven't devoted the time and attention required to understand how their firm creates value. They simply assume that trying hard and "being your best" are the keys to success. But just as "hope is not a strategy," trying hard is not a strategy, either.

You can begin to understand points of relevance and points of difference by applying both analytical and creative thinking to questions like:

- What business categories or industry segments do we know best?
- What kinds of clients have we been successful in attracting in the past?
- Which client stakeholders do we know best?
- What differentiating methods and approaches do we use?
- What kind of special knowledge and expertise do we possess?

NOT SERVICE, BUT KNOWLEDGE

Service is a commodity. Smart thinking is not. Clients can get good service anywhere, but proactive thought leadership is in short supply. In fact, many surveys that seek to diagnose why clients switch firms, produce the same answer: "Because our firm never gave us anything we didn't ask for."

So throughout this book I will use the language professional *knowledge* firm wherever possible, because clients don't hire you just for what you do, but rather for what you *know*.

In an effort to practice what I preach, I'm writing this book from the perspective of what I know best: marketing firms. While the principles and practices in this book apply just as much to a law firm as to an advertising agency, most of the specific examples I give come from my area of focus and expertise. Before forming Ignition Consulting Group, I spent several decades working in the advertising agency business, both at large multi-national firms and as a CEO and partner of mid-sized firms. This experience of working at both ends of the size spectrum has informed my current work as a consultant to marketing firms of all shapes and sizes both here and abroad.

While I come from a family of academics, mine is a much more practical approach: the product of years of helping professional firms define them-selves. It's ironic to think that even branding firms usually need help defining their own brand, but it is precisely this kind of work that has allowed me to develop the body of intellectual capital contained in this book. Once you've made it through the 10 chapters, look to the appendices at the back of the book—these can be used to measure your firm's success at differentiating itself, whether you're part of a start-up or a developed business. Additional information is available at www.positioningforprofessionals.com.

If the methods in *Positioning for Professionals* can work for even the toughest cases (firms like advertising agencies that brand their clients but have a difficult time branding themselves), there's a very good chance they can work for all other sorts of professional knowledge firms.

Tim Williams
Salt Lake City, Utah
March 2010

Size Is Not a Strategy

I n the past 20 years, no marketing concept has captured the collective business imagination more than "branding." Every year, several important new books are written on the subject. And professional service firms from business consultancies to advertising agencies are advising clients on how to "brand" their offering.

Given the billions invested in this effort, it's worth stepping back to examine the nature and value of brands. In answer to the question, "Why is a strong brand important?" one might say that it creates customer preference, lifts sales, or even makes the sales force's job easier. But the most important answer to this question is that *a brand commands a higher price*. And the stronger the brand, the higher the price.

This phenomenon is indisputable; it's been demonstrated numerous times by research and brand consultancies the world over. In one such recent study, international research firm Millward Brown looked at a variety of brands of differing sizes and indexed their price against the category. What they found, not surprisingly, is that "it is abundantly clear that brands with higher equity have a price premium over lower equity brands"[1] (see Figure 1.1).

1

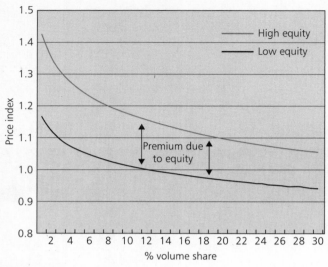

Figure 1.1   The High-Equity Price Differential
Source: Adapted from "Brand Equity and the Bottom Line," by Peter Walshe ánd Helen Fearn, *Admap*, March 2008.

Now consider the seemingly naïve question, "What's the value of a higher price?" The answer is higher profits for the company that markets the brand.

Profit is the reason companies are in business—not sales, not revenues, not growth, but profit. And one thing trumps all others in the business mix when it comes to profitability: the pricing integrity of the brand.

MAINTAINING PRICING INTEGRITY

The investment companies make in "branding" is not just to sell more, but ultimately to decrease customers' sensitivity to price. In fact, it could be argued that the default purpose of marketing is not to increase sales but rather to increase profits. More than anything else, profit is a direct result of protecting pricing integrity through powerful brand differentiation.

Even marketing programs that don't do much to boost revenues can increase margins by differentiating brands and thus allowing companies to raise prices. In other words, while brand-building efforts may not always increase revenues in the short term, they produce the important result of allowing the brand to charge higher prices over the long term.

The value of premium pricing is significant. A study by McKinsey shows that reducing costs improves a company's profits only marginally, whereas increasing the brand's price improves profits dramatically. A 5 percent improvement in price can result in as much as a 50 percent improvement in profits.[2]

Says the author of *Priceless*, an exploration of the power of pricing, "Because profit margins are small to begin with, adding a percent or two can boost profits immensely. Very few interventions can have such an effect on the bottom line."[3]

Nothing can improve a company's bottom line better than protecting and enhancing its ability to command a higher price. This means that revenues are not the key metric of your firm's success; profits are. Profit is driven mostly by price. Price is driven mostly by brand perception. This makes brand building an activity central to the success of every professional firm.

BETTER TO BE A PROFIT LEADER THAN A MARKET LEADER

Sadly, growth for the sake of growth has become enshrined as the goal of business. Wall Street wants its growth projections, and any company that is not consistently increasing market share is seen as an investment risk.

There are, of course, different *kinds* of growth: growth in sales, growth in market share, growth in market penetration, and so on. However, the only growth that really matters is growth in profitability. It's easy to grow sales and market share and still be unprofitable. Companies—not just some, but *most* companies, including professional firms—routinely "buy" sales and market share by discounting. That kind of growth isn't growth at all; it's merely a form of unhealthy enlargement.

"Fixating on market share instead of profits actually tends to decrease profitability," says Wharton's J. Scott Armstrong. Former *Wall Street Journal* editor Richard Miniter argues that market share is "the fool's gold of business."[4] A lot of commonly accepted assumptions about bigness are simply not true. A few of them are shown in Table 1.1.

What moral can be learned from this comparison of the assumptions versus the reality? Companies should be concerned with profit leadership, not market share leadership.

Table 1.1   The Myths of Bigness

The Assumption	The Reality
Size creates pricing power.	The largest companies in the category are usually the first both to lower and match prices of competitors. They are also the most likely to use discounting and couponing as a tactic to buy more (unprofitable) market share. The bigger the company, the bigger the losses resulting from price wars. As most executives have learned, in a price war nobody wins. The only way a large company can create pricing power is the same way small companies do it: by creating and nurturing a highly differentiated brand.
The largest companies benefit from higher economies of scale.	Because of overdiversification, most large companies actually experience "diseconomies" of scale. It typically costs much more to serve the needs of a broad, mass market than it does a narrow, focused market. Larger companies also tend to have larger hierarchies that create significantly more overhead. The fallacy of the "efficiency" argument also applies to professional services. How many professional firms achieve twice the efficiencies with twice as many associates?
The largest companies attract and keep the best management talent.	The largest public companies almost always have the lowest return on assets, not the highest. They are also the most likely to be saddled with debt from unsuccessful mergers and acquisitions, usually resulting from an unhealthy obsession with being the biggest company in the category.
Size leads to profitability.	Actually, three times out of four the most profitable firm is *not* the one with the largest slice of the market.

WHY BIGNESS DOESN'T LEAD TO GREATNESS

Jim Collins describes the stages through which successful companies pass on the way to their downfall. Second on the list: the undisciplined pursuit of more.[5] Growth through acquisition—pursuing more for the sake of more—is usually an unsuccessful strategy. The majority of mergers and acquisitions fail, and sometimes spectacularly so (think DaimlerChrysler and AOL/TimeWarner). While some of these attempted partnerships build the CEO's ego, they usually erode shareholder value.

Most business books feature examples of publicly owned companies, which largely have shaped the collective consciousness of the business community. We have come to accept business axioms (such as "grow or die") that apply mostly to companies that are in a constant quest to satisfy shareholders. But privately held companies—which actually make up the majority of businesses—can and usually do operate under a different set of principles.[6]

The most exceptional private companies have chosen not to focus on revenue growth but rather to be the best at what they do. Many in fact place significant limits on their growth, choosing instead to focus on doing great work, providing great service, and creating a great place to work.

In professional services, the largest firm is seldom if ever the best. In the advertising world, one of the firm's with the best reputation, the best pricing power, and the best work is far from being the largest. Crispin Porter + Bogusky employs fewer than 1,000 people (compared with the multinational agencies that employ tens of thousands), yet repeatedly has been named "Agency of the Year" by leading trade publications and business organizations. As is so often the case, the best firm in the category isn't marginally better, but significantly outperforms other firms in the industry. In a recent annual compilation of worldwide creative awards, CP+B earned almost twice as many awards as the second-place firm. The gulf between the best and the rest is reflected in the observation of admen Jonathan Bond and Richard Kirshenbaum, who believe that "there are perhaps as few as 40 or 50 agencies in the United States that can actually manufacture a good campaign, and possibly 10 that do it consistently."[7]

HIRED TO BE EFFECTIVE, NOT EFFICIENT

Advertising Age observes, "The list of great brands that have been damaged, even ruined, as they've been milked for growth rather than managed for profit is a long one—and it grows every year."[8]

The unbridled quest for growth has played out in very visible ways in the marketing communications industry. Today, just five holding companies control 85 percent of the advertising expenditures in the world. In addition to creating leverage when negotiating media contracts, this roll up of marketing communications companies also was expected to produce significant economies of scale. It didn't. What was the total "savings" resulting from consolidating the operations of thousands of agencies? It was less than .025 percent.[9]

The goal of professional knowledge firms should not be efficiency, but rather effectiveness. Can you imagine choosing a doctor based on efficiency instead of effectiveness? Tax advisors, lawyers, and marketing consultants are (or should be) hired for the same reasons. What's ultimately important isn't how hard you try or how many hours you spend, but rather whether you win the case, successfully keep a client out of tax trouble, or create more equity for your client's brand.

Bad Clients Drive Out Good Clients

If the goal is greatness, not bigness, it follows that what professional firms need is not more business, but better business. My colleague Ron Baker has coined a truth he calls "Baker's law": Bad clients drive out good clients.

What is a "bad client?" A bad client is a low-value client, one that doesn't add any value to the firm's bottom line, professional satisfaction, or reputation.

- Low-value clients are unprofitable. There is simply no rational argument for keeping an unprofitable client. Look at your firm's financials and you'll likely see Pareto's law in effect: 20 percent of your clients generate 80 percent of your income and profit. Generally speaking, about one-third of a firm's clients actually *cost* the firm money.

- Low-value clients usually run your team ragged because they're poorly organized, have unreasonable approval processes, and constantly change direction because they're not focused enough to give the firm good input and clear direction.

- Low-value clients often treat your team with lack of respect, thereby creating a relationship characterized by lack of collaboration, mediocre work, and strained nerves.

So why are so many firms filled with clients that fit this description? The excuse offered up by most principals is, "They at least help cover our overhead." They have the attitude that every dollar is a good dollar. But some dollars actually have *negative* value when the result is demoralized people who leave for other jobs and a damaged agency reputation that hurts prospecting efforts for both people and clients.

Not every dollar is a good dollar. The only kind of growth you should want is smart growth. Income is vanity, but profit is sanity. Here's an effective way to determine who your best clients are:

- Earn profit of at least 20 percent
- Treat team with respect
- Provide timely, constructive feedback
- Openly provide and make available important and relevant information and data
- Involve appropriate decision makers and allow access to senior-level executives
- Be able to articulate the outcomes the firm's work is expected to produce
- Be willing to consider unconventional solutions and approaches
- Encourage and approve quality work
- Provide clear direction that minimizes false starts and changes
- Coordinate effectively with other departments within the client organization
- Allow time for the firm to do its best work
- Involve the firm in relevant meetings and decision making
- Attempt to resolve differences with the firm fairly
- Be willing to test new approaches and take calculated risks
- Have good growth potential as a client

One brilliant way to get rid of your low-value clients is to charge them the highest price. Ironically, most low-value clients end up getting our lowest price, because they complain the most. Do just the opposite and your low-value clients will disappear.

Not only is growth not a strategy, but the supposed advantages of size are diminishing, especially in professional services. Aside from the benefits of what could be considered reputational capital, "bigness" is no longer a competitive advantage for law, accounting, advertising, or consulting. In fact, the trend is clearly away from big diversified firms to smaller specialized operations. In the paper "The Death of Big Law," Larry Ribstein chronicles the megatrends behind the devolution of large law firms, including increased access to legal information and resources via technology, competition from lower cost economies, and the "commoditization" of some forms of legal work that are widely available on legal websites.[10]

In the following chapter, we look at how and why products and services become commoditized, and the remedies for professional knowledge brands.

CHAPTER 2

How and Why Brands Become Homogenized

In every category, it's virtually inevitable that the brands (and companies that market them) will become more and more alike. In the seamlessly connected world of digital communications, this phenomenon is both accelerated and exaggerated. Studies show that an increasing number of categories are becoming more commodity-like in the eyes of consumers. In categories ranging from insurance to legal services, brands are seen as becoming less differentiated.[1]

In mature markets, competition drives up quality and convenience to a point where many brands begin to look like commodities. Products and product features are mostly copied rather than invented. Copying is perceived as less risky, and risk is what most humans strenuously seek to avoid. There is, of course, an important difference between real risk and perceived risk; in marketing the real risk is simply copying what other brands do. Copying leads to undifferentiated brands, commoditization of entire categories, and erosion of pricing power.

Copying also diverts companies and brands from doing what they do best and instead puts them on "the long road to unfocus."[2] There is no competitive advantage in doing simply what others do or, worse, attempting to do *everything* others do.

A general hospital that does a little bit of everything must support a huge staff of various kinds of professionals and a wide variety of equipment and supplies. The result, as Harvard's Clayton Christensen points out, "is not just a lack of differentiation but dissatisfaction." By attempting to do a lot of things well, they end up doing nothing really well.[3] Compare that with the hospital with a specialized focus that is able to deliver superior service by marshalling and integrating just the right people, equipment, and resources to treat a specific kind of disease. Christensen and his colleagues equate brand positioning with the idea of "hiring" a product, service, or company to do a particular job. Not all jobs, just a very specific job. And the more specific the job, the better.

> Focusing a product and its brand on a job creates differentiation. The rub, however, is that when a company communicates the job a branded product was designed to do perfectly, it is also communicating what jobs the product should not be hired to do. Focus is scary—at least the carmakers seem to think so. They deliberately create words as brands that have no meaning in any language, with no tie to any job, in the myopic hope that each individual model will be hired by every customer for every job. In the face of compelling evidence that purpose-branded products that do specific jobs well command premium pricing and compete in markets that are much larger than those defined by product categories, the automakers' products are substantially undifferentiated, the average subbrand commands less than a 1 percent market share, and most automakers are losing money. Somebody gave these folks the wrong recipe for prosperity.[4]

THE URGE TO COPY

Counterfeiting of branded goods is now a $250 billion business, according to the International Anticounterfeiting Coalition. While most firms obviously wouldn't do something as blatant (and illegal) as literally copying another company's product, they won't hesitate to copy another company's business strategy.

The temptation to copy in business is irresistible. Business leaders logically conclude they can replicate another company's success by duplicating their attributes and capabilities. This is what makes the concepts of "benchmarking" and "best practices" so pernicious. They just encourage one company to adopt another's business practices.

As the advertising agency for Apple, TBWA/Chiat/Day says on the home page of their website, "Copying is always easier than deciding if and when to change. But what if there was a way to identify and disrupt the limits to your success?"[5]

Because most enterprises haven't taken the time or exercised the will-power to define a relevant, differentiating value proposition of their own, they default to the nonstrategy of adaptation—adaptation of category features, benefits, and pricing. They simply adapt to the status quo in the category. But powerful value propositions are never the result of duplicating what other brands or companies do. In fact, they're often born out of doing the exact opposite.

THE FOLLY OF ALL-IN-ONE

One of the main forces at play that leads brands to become homogeneous is the tendency to define the value proposition solely in terms of product or service attributes. Believing that the more product attributes a brand can claim, the more valuable it will be to the customer, brands continue to add more and more features until they become "all-in-one solutions."

The problem is, of course, nobody buys a product or service because it can do everything, but rather because it can do *something*. Nowhere is this more apparent than in packaged goods, where many categories ultimately produce a "total solution" brand. Witness Colgate Total, Crest Complete, Olay Total Effects, and Tide Total Care. Can a laundry detergent really stand for protecting color, enhancing softness, cleaning thoroughly, fighting stains, and preserving fabrics? After years of marching down the "complete" path, P&G is realizing that a single-benefit brand is often stronger for the simple reason that it stands for something. It promises to do a specific job extremely well instead of attempting to do a lot of jobs moderately well. What's true for packaged goods is true for professional services as well as every other type of brand.

LINE EXTENSION IS NOT BRANDING

In marketing, the most obvious form of copying is line extension—extending the name of an existing brand onto a new brand. Line extension is tempting because brand owners believe it will spare them the expense of creating an entirely new brand name. But experience shows that a line extension inevitably cannibalizes the sales of the "parent" brand. And it always produces confusion around what the brand name means in the first place.

No one is more outspoken about the evils of line extensions than business strategist Al Ries, who has documented scores of examples of what he calls "the hockey stick effect." Imagine a hockey stick as a graph. Short term, a line extension can score some goals, which produces the "blade." But long term, says Ries, "you get the shaft."

Take the example of Budweiser's seemingly successful introduction of Bud Light, which for the first few years didn't hurt the sales of the flagship Budweiser beer brand. But then the hockey stick effect came into play. Total Budweiser volume has fallen every year for 20 years. The long-term effects of line extensions are underobserved and underreported by the business and marketing press. What's true for Budweiser is true for literally hundreds of other line-extended brands from soda to batteries to professional services.[6]

Line extension is perhaps the most pernicious form of copying. Besides being built on the faulty belief that the line extension can flourish without affecting the core brand, it's a severe form of laziness. Companies that attempt to extend an already-successful brand name and reputation onto another product are showing the same lack of innovation that creates weak brands in the first place.

Some companies attempt a form of line extension that could be considered a "supermarket strategy," which aims to apply the same brand name to literally thousands of products and services. This approach, attempted most notably by the big Japanese and Korean conglomerates, has proven to be a huge profit drain. By pursuing short-term revenues through expansion and line extension, companies like Panasonic, Hitachi, Sharp, NEC, Sanyo, Fujitsu, and even Sony all began a serious profit slide long before the recession of 2008 took effect.

Overdiversification has led these previously successful companies to expand well beyond what they can do well. Visit almost any electronics or home appliance store and you'll see everything from cell phones to microwaves carrying the logos of these conglomerates. Some are in literally hundreds of businesses.

For example, what does the brand name Hitachi mean? Apparently it's meant to stand for refrigerators, microwaves, bread makers, garbage disposals, washing machines, vacuum cleaners, irons, batteries, lamps, hair dryers, face shavers, room air conditioners, dehumidifiers, electric fans, televisions, projectors, camcorders, DVD players, computers, mobile phones, home elevators, ventilation systems, boilers, pumps, power tools, garden supplies, travel, finance, software, servers, information security systems, building security, semiconductors, automotive equipment, chemical materials, cable, logistics systems, railroad solutions, medical devices, animation software, power generation, and construction equipment. Whew!

Executives of companies like these misunderstand the fact that brands usually can own only one category at a time. A business model centered on building revenues instead of building brands almost always will lead a company in this same dead-end direction.

THERE'S NO SUCH THING AS FULL SERVICE

There's no such thing as full service. There isn't a brand in any category that actually can fulfill every need, but that doesn't stop thousands of professional firms from claiming it. The promise of full service seems almost to be the perceived price of entry. Read the first sentence of the home page of the professional knowledge firms in your city and you'll likely find the words "full service."

Even many of the highly specialized firms can't resist preceding a description of their specialty with the words "full service," as in, "Marshall & Pine is a full-service advertising agency with an expertise in direct response television," or, "The Lake Partnership is a full-service law firm specializing in divorce law." Perish the thought that you might be getting half service when you hire one of these firms.

The full-service promise often is accompanied by other undifferentiating terms like "wide range," "full line," and "complete." Imagine that you're a corporation having tax troubles with the IRS. Would you be looking for a "full-service law firm with a wide range of experience in a variety of industries," or would you prefer a firm with deep expertise in corporate tax law? No client ever buys a "wide range of expertise," but rather a specific kind of expertise. Imagine hiring a "visual artist with a wide range of photographic experience" when what you really want is a good wedding photographer.

Try to discern the value proposition of this firm, taken from an actual advertising agency website:

> We draw on a wide array of disciplines, fueled by strategy and creativity. Every communication is targeted to meet strategic goals and deliver more value in the process. . . . From a wide spectrum of disciplines, we determine the right solution set. . . . In short, we have no preconceived ideas of what will work in any situation, so we bring every tool, every experience, every talent to bear on every assignment. This open approach gives us the freedom to do what's right for our clients. And that looks different for every one of them.

Whenever "wide range" or full service appears as the main promise a company makes, you can assume that it has been either unable or unwilling to actually name what it stands for.

THE NATURAL FEAR OF FOCUS

Marketers fear focus for myriad reasons, but the leading fear is the belief that if they focus their brand to solve a particular problem, they won't be solving other problems, thereby making the brand less appealing to everyone. But brands are not marketed to "everyone." A product—a laptop computer—might be bought by "everyone," but a brand—the Panasonic Tough Book—is purchased by a very specific kind of customer looking for a specific job to be done.

By appealing to everyone, brands end up appealing to no one. Standing for everything is the same as standing for nothing.

Attempting to offer a comprehensive "bundled solution" to customers is really what could be considered false bundling because it usually lacks a strategy. Strategic bundling of core services to a targeted customer can be effective, particularly when it comes to pricing. But an unfocused collection of every possible service a customer might want or need is not bundling at all—it's mostly just overwhelming.

In workshops around the country the author asks advertising executives to articulate their "elevator pitch." In other words, how would they describe their firm in a relevant, differentiating way during the 30 seconds it takes for a typical elevator ride?

Some typical responses are:

- We are a fully integrated marketing communications firm that propels businesses with unusually intelligent and creative solutions.
- We are an integrated full-service agency that challenges the status quo of clients to move them beyond the norm.
- We are a full-service, fully integrated marketing firm that combines best-in-class capabilities with the personal attention of an entrepreneurial partner. We measure our success on the results we help achieve for our clients.
- We are a marketing solutions company that creates ideas that move products and services with heart and determination.
- We are smart, insight-driven partners obsessed with improving our clients' business.
- We are an open partner who wants to be a champion of your brand—to grow it, expand it, and evolve it. You success is our success.
- We are a team of innovative thinkers across all disciplines of marketing communications—planning, research, execution, and evaluation—delivered with passion and enthusiasm.

There are literally hundreds more where these came from. This presents a pretty sad commentary on the industry that is in the business of creating brands.

The problem isn't that these positionings lack style (which they do), but rather that they lack *substance*. They fail to reflect an understanding that a positioning strategy is a declaration of where the firm intends to play in the marketplace. Positioning means deciding not only what business you're in, but what business you're *not* in.

Shreddies: The Power of Perceived Differentiation

Even the *perception* of a differentiated product can have powerful effects in the marketplace, and even with a product as commonplace as breakfast cereal.

In Canada a breakfast cereal called Shreddies—little squares of shredded wheat—made a comeback after the advertising agency had the idea to advertise them as "new diamond Shreddies."

New advertising showed the little squares of wheat turned on a 45-degree angle, producing a false but remarkably effective product innovation. The advertising agency, Ogilvy & Mather Toronto, served up a package redesign, advertising, and publicity to draw people to diamondshreddies.com for recipes, a chance to win a diamond, an interactive game, and videos of actual focus groups testing the product using a comedian as the moderator.

In stores, surprised shoppers found Diamond Shreddies, and these limited-edition boxes sold out in just two months. An online debate quickly ensued with customers wondering whether or not the repackaging was a joke. One fan even put "the last square Shreddie" for sale on eBay. The parent company, Post, reported a drastic lift in sales and the campaign won a Grand Clio.

The *perception* of the brand is what makes the brand. For years, blind taste tests between Pepsi and Coke have put Pepsi consistently on top. But the strength of the Coca-Cola brand allows it to outsell Pepsi by 50 percent in the United States. You don't always make a brand more successful by making it better, but by making it *different*.

CHAPTER 3

The Mature Company's Identity Crisis

I n mature or "developed" categories where brands have been making steady incremental feature improvements, the category usually reaches a stage that could be considered "excess performance." It's at this point that most of the brands in the category become "commoditized" in the sense that they all deliver the same main category benefits. This makes it difficult to differentiate between brands, and therefore customers become unwilling to pay any kind of premium for one brand over another. Worse, as these brands continue to introduce more incremental improvements, customers are unwilling to pay more for these features, since the brands already "overdeliver."

Economists teach that when the marginal increase in price that a company can derive from product or service improvements reaches zero, then the incremental usefulness of the improvements is also zero. This is the world in which most mature brands—including professional service brands—find themselves; they risk being overpriced by virtue of being underexclusive.

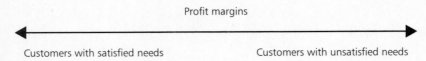

Figure 3.1 Different Value Propositions, Different Cost Structures

The strategic choice you have is to serve either customers with unsatisfied needs in higher tiers of the market, or customers with largely satisfied needs in lower tiers of the market. These are two very different value propositions (which are discussed in detail later in the book), with very different cost structures and profit margins[1] (see Figure 3.1.).

DIFFERENTIATION AND PRICE PREMIUMS

In mature, homogeneous categories the basis of competition defaults primarily to cost. There are really few other factors upon which customers or clients can base their purchase decision. When brands in a category attempt to compete mostly on price, it's a sign of an undifferentiated marketplace. Lack of pricing power correlates directly to lack of a differentiating value proposition.

Michael Porter has argued that there are really only two essential business strategies: low cost and differentiation.[2] Some brands that have a low-cost strategy—most notably the low-cost airlines—have chosen cost as a deliberate strategy supported by a disruptive business model that produces cost efficiencies that competitors can't match. In the world of professional services, examples would include online legal services such as LegalZoom, H&R Block's online tax preparation service, or SpotRunner, an online service that lets marketers create their own TV ads.

But most of the brands that are competing on price arrived there by *default* rather than by design. They find themselves in price wars because they have failed to select a valuable spot on the value chain. They have allowed themselves to be pushed along the chain with their competitors until all of the brands in the category are saying the same things, offering the same features, and making incremental improvements that customers are largely unwilling to pay for. This is not a very envious position to be in for any company.

David Baker, who consults for the creative services industry, puts it this way: "When you do everything for everybody, the only leverage you have is doing more of it faster and cheaper."[3]

As we've discussed, getting a better price is the essential advantage of a brand over a commodity. Premium priced brands like the Apple iPhone, the Porsche 911, the Montblanc fountain pen, and the Stihl chainsaw all do a specific job in ways that other less-focused brands do not and cannot. And that is the reason they are all able to carry a significant price premium over other brands in their categories.

In fact, one well-known methodology, Young & Rubicam's Brand Asset Evaluator, shows that strongly differentiated brands financially out-perform less differentiated competitors in three key areas: profit margin (+50 percent), market cap growth (+250 percent), and operating earn-ings (+270 percent).[4] The top 100 brands as identified by the consultancy Interbrand consistently and significantly have outperformed the S&P 500. In fact, the performance gulf between the top brands and all the rest has only grown, not diminished, during the "Great Recession" that started in 2008.

COLUMBUS, NOT NAPOLEON

Defining a differentiating value proposition requires that we stop focusing on reclaiming old territory and instead discover *new* territory. The model is Columbus, not Napoleon. Most firms are engaged in fighting "turf wars" instead of finding new turf.

Turf wars often manifest themselves as pricing wars. In professional firms this is more discreet than in manufacturing, but these price wars exist nonetheless. Witness the rise of procurement's role in selecting some pro-fessional services, particularly advertising agencies. As most mass marketers know, when brands engage in price wars, the result is that everyone loses. When procurement forces a price war among professional firms, the only winter is procurement.

Because of the urge to copy and the tendency to imitate, many industries are mimicking what economists call "perfect competition." While true per-fect competition is more theory than reality, it comes closest to existing in categories like farmers markets, generic pharmaceuticals, and free software. Today's overcrowded professional services marketplace sometimes looks like "near-perfect competition" because it meets so many of the theoretical requirements, including:

- **Homogeneous products and services:** The characteristics of the product or service do not vary much across providers.
- **Industry-standard specifications:** The means of developing the product or service are well understood and widely available.
- **Excess supply of buyers and sellers:** There are an abundance of customers with the willingness and ability to buy the product or service at a certain price, and an abundance of producers with the willingness and ability to supply the product at a certain price.
- **Wide availability:** There is overcapacity in the market because the product or service is widely distributed and easily obtained.
- **Low barriers to entry and exit:** It is relatively easy for a business to enter or exit the market.
- **Total access to information:** Prices and quality of products are widely known to customers and producers.
- **Low transaction costs:** Buyers and sellers incur low costs in making an exchange.
- **The customer is in control:** Because the product is largely the same and customers have access to information, the customer has a large degree of leverage in the purchase process.

The opposite of perfect competition is monopolistic competition. Economic theory states that commoditization is what happens when a market moves from a state of monopolistic competition to one of perfect competition. A product essentially becomes perceived as a commodity when customers perceive little or no value difference between brands or versions.

It may be hard to imagine that the professional services industry could be skirting on the edge of perfect competition (ironically, advertising agencies

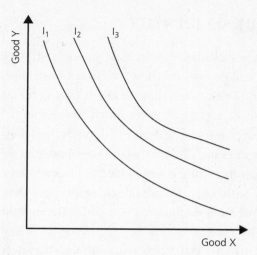

Figure 3.2 The Indifference Curve

may be at the top of the list). But there are many worrisome signs that they are headed in this direction: Many prospective clients develop spreadsheets designed to carefully compare the costs of one firm against another. Firms get lined up and "shopped" based on hourly rates. But the most troubling trend of all is that procurement agents—often the exact same people who buy office supplies—are now primary decision makers in hiring many types of professional service firms.

With these dynamics happening in the marketplace, it's easy to start believing that efficiency is what you're selling (and the procurement community certainly does its best to reinforce this). But as Adam Smith taught back in 1776, in mature markets profits don't come from increased efficiency (which is the traditional management mindset) but rather from increased innovation and differentiation.

Undifferentiated products, services, and companies fall on what economists call the "indifference curve," a graph showing groups of offerings to which the consumer is literally indifferent. At each point of an indifference curve, the consumer has no preference for one offering over another (see Figure 3.2). This is not a very desirable place to be.

THE DIFFUSION OF IDENTITY

Ask business executives about their most pressing strategic imperatives and cost-cutting will be high on their list. They obsess much more about lowering the brand's price than they do about raising the brand's perception. Company leaders tend to exert much more energy in improving operating efficiencies and strong-arming suppliers than they do in making their brand more relevant, differentiated, and valuable to their customers. What's true in manufacturing is just as true in professional services.

The problem with most brands, once again, isn't that they're overpriced. They're just underexclusive. Price and differentiation are directly correlated.

If leaders of professional firms truly embraced differentiation as a strategy, we would see actions and consequences such as those shown in Table 3.1.

LANDING IN NO-MAN'S LAND

If you're not out to be one of the low cost leaders, then you'd better commit to a strategy that transcends matching or beating your competitors' price. The goal is to protect your price—not lower it—and strong brand differentiation is the only road that will take you there.

Table 3.1   Being Different

Most Firms Do This	A Firm That Embraces Differentiation Does This
Describe their firm using language that is remarkably similar in both style and substance	Use different language to describe itself
Mimic the structure of other firms in their category, with virtually identical business models	Have a different structure and business model
Prospect for exactly the same clients (everybody with money)	Prospect for a very specific type of client that matches a specific positioning and focus
Price their services in exactly the same way (in fact, going out of their way to make sure their "hourly rates" are at a parity with other firms)	Price their services differently (and creatively)

Table 3.2   Low Cost versus High Value

	Offering	Brand Promise	Operational Approach	Marketing Approach
Low-Cost Strategy	Widely available products and services	Cost, efficiency, help save money	Control expenses, make full use of assets, manage capacity, reduce errors	Level the playing field; make it easy for customers and clients to compare
High-Value Strategy	Specialized products and services; not widely available	Outcomes, effectiveness, help make money	Align expectations, assign the right talent, leverage knowledge and experience	Unlevel the playing field; make it difficult for customers to compare

If your business *is* based on a genuine low-cost strategy, then by all means you should be investing a lot of your creativity in making your brand as inexpensive as possible. Just remember that there can be only one low-cost leader in any category. At the other end of the spectrum are the high-price brands, competing on a strategy of differentiation. Of course the middle of the spectrum is where you find most brands; that no-man's land of brands that are neither low cost nor different—the mediocre middle.

Table 3.2 shows how and why these are two very different strategies.

The company brands at either end of the spectrum generally do well. It's the brands in the middle that struggle. You have to pick one strategy or the other. As Confucius said, "Man who chases two rabbits catches neither."

STRATEGY AT THE EDGES

Statistically speaking, the concept of "average" means that you fall right in the middle of the bell curve. No company wants to be thought of as just average, yet that is precisely where their undifferentiated business strategy places them—in the center of the curve. The most interesting and powerful brands are at the edges of the bell curve, because they're doing things differently.

It feels like common sense to play in the center of the market, but the middle is actually the least desirable place to be. If you try to simultaneously appeal to the high end of the market and the low end of the market, guess where you end up? You'll end up in the "mushy middle," where you appeal to no market.

Look at most markets and there are examples of successful brands at the high end and low end, but very few successful brands in the middle (like the curve in Figure 3.3). This is most visible in retailing, where there is almost no middle market at all. Trying to make The Gap a middle-market brand essentially killed it, while Banana Republic at the higher end and Old Navy at the lower end are doing well. In kitchen appliances, brands like Viking and Wolf are thriving, along with the more affordable LG line, but the brands in the middle like Maytag are struggling.[5]

Marketing to the middle was the essential mistake of General Motors. This phenomenon is true even in real estate, where high-end and entry-level properties are the ones that sell even in difficult markets.

Brands that follow a "best of both worlds" strategy—selling to the middle—will never be the most famous, the most profitable, or the most successful. This is a doomed strategy even in politics. Moderates seldom win elections. "Moderates," says the controversial commentator Rush Limbaugh, "by definition have no principles."

The Economist reports on what it calls the "middle-class struggle," the phenomenon in which the media world is divided into blockbusters and

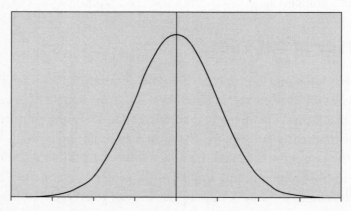

Figure 3.3   The Middle Just Means Average

niches—with everything else in between struggling. This is true of everything from movies to television to newspapers.[6]

Margin in Mystery

When you think about it, selling primarily on the basis of price is the direct opposite of selling based on the reputation of the brand. Commanding a higher price is the essence of what it means to be a brand. Producers of unbranded pork bellies sell their products on the Chicago Mercantile Exchange at the same price on the same day. But Hormel hams sell at a significant price premium over other brands in the meat section of the supermarket. Is Hormel's pork *product* that much better than other pork products? Maybe. But their *brand* certainly is.

Brands sell on the basis of perceived value, not costs. This is what makes the hourly rate such a pernicious concept. It's based on a formula of salary costs plus overhead plus desired profit, which has nothing to do with the value an hour actually produces for the client. (See Chapter 10 for much more on this topic.)

What are the areas where clients are the *most* price sensitive? Things that clients believe they could do themselves if they wanted to devote the time and resources. What are the areas where clients are the *least* price sensitive? Services and capabilities that clients can't do on their own, or could do only at great expense and disruption to their business model.

Taken one step further, the products and services that can command the absolute highest prices are those that the client could never duplicate, no matter how much time and money the client threw at them. Here we enter the realm of proprietary approaches, methodologies, and forms of intellectual capital that are truly unique to the firm.

NOT BEST PRACTICES, BUT NEXT PRACTICES

Rather than investing their time and energy into differentiating, most firms are busy benchmarking. The practice of benchmarking—learning how other companies do something—is mostly imitation. It produces what could be called a world of karaoke companies, where one company mimics another. Say the authors of *Karaoke Capitalism*:

> Our world is full of karaoke companies. In business there are even names for this imitation frenzy; benchmarking and best practice—as if these fancy labels would make a difference. Let's face it, no matter what the pundits say, benchmarking will never get you to the top—merely to the middle.[7]

Benchmarking other brands or companies is nothing more than institutionalized imitation. Sometimes imitation is not only intentional, but is actually a business strategy, like the recreations of Paris and Venice on the Las Vegas strip. Unfortunately, most imitation is *unintentional*—the result of unoriginal thinking and lack of imagination.

Look up the definition of the word *remarkable*: "worth noticing or commenting on." That's a good standard for your firm. What's different enough about what you do that's worth noticing or commenting on? The most "remarkable" brands are in fact the ones that get talked about the most. A new database called the Engagementdb (www.engagementdb. com) ranks the most talked about brands. Not surprisingly, companies like Starbucks, Nike, and Apple—all remarkable brands—rank near the top. In today's socially networked business world, it could be argued that an active, positive online reputation is one of your firm's most valuable strategic assets. The key, of course, is that your firm must be worth talking about. A middle-of-the-road, standing-for-everything positioning strategy is unlikely to get you there.

Simply mirroring what other firms do, is not only a strategic but a tactical mistake. Your job as the leader of a professional knowledge firm is to unlevel the playing field; to make it difficult to compare your firm with others. Behavioral psychology tells us that the way to be truly "incomparable" is to avoid offering the commonplace. Using consumer package goods as an example, if you as a consumer were asked the average price of a gallon of milk, you'd have a pretty good answer. What would you expect to pay for a bottle of white truffle oil? Because it's an uncommon item, most of us wouldn't have an accurate guess. Professional knowledge firms that offer up the standard list of services and capabilities are therefore quite "comparable" with other firms.

In new business situations, most firms attempt to answer this challenge by saying that their work is better than other firms', and that's what makes them different. But simply being better isn't different. Only different is different.

CHAPTER 4

Expanding Your Business By Narrowing Your Focus

C ompanies of all stripes make the mistake of assuming that narrow is the same thing as small; that if you're focused in one area, you somehow limit your growth potential.

While seemingly logical, this is simply not true. Starbucks is narrow—coffee—but it certainly isn't small. Intel is narrow—mostly microchips—but ranks as a Fortune 500 company. In professional services, some of the largest firms are some of the most focused. For example, while most other advertising agencies attempt to position themselves as "full service," a firm called Zimmerman headquartered in Orlando, Florida, is focused on the retail category. The firm calls its specialization "brandtailing," which it defines as the combination of strong expertise in both branding and retailing. As far as ad agencies go, this is a pretty "narrow" focus. But the result is anything but small. With billings of around $2.5 billion, Zimmerman employs several thousand people.

Table 4.1   Narrow Is Not Small

Marketing Communications Firm	Focus	U.S. Revenue
Acxiom	Direct marketing	$632,000,000
Razorfish	Digital marketing	$317,000,000
Carlson Marketing	Promotional marketing	$172,000,000
CommonHealth	Healthcare marketing	$141,000,000
InterBrand	Branding & identity	$120,000,000
iCrossing	Search marketing	$79,000,000
Dieste	Hispanic marketing	$45,000,000

Table 4.1 shows some other examples from the world of marketing firms.

Of the top 25 advertising agencies in America, more than 60% are specialist firms, not "full-service" agencies. In Minneapolis, a city that has spawned more than its share of talented advertising agencies over the past few decades, the largest agency is not Fallon or Campbell Mithun—firms that help put Minneapolis on the advertising map—but rather Carlson Marketing, a specialist in customer relationship marketing. With revenues of some $265 million, Carlson Marketing is nearly four times larger than any other agency in the city.

The fact is that the road to profitability is paved with strong value propositions in which a company makes a specific promise to a specific customer. Tom's of Maine promises completely natural oral care to a core group of people who are health and environment conscious and commands a 30 percent price premium over other oral care products. A narrow target doesn't mean narrow profits. In fact, a niche market almost always returns higher margins than a mass market because the brand meets a very specific set of needs.

Instead of being afraid of focus, you should be afraid of mediocrity.

THERE'S NO SUCH THING AS A GENERAL MARKET

Logic would suggest that you'll grow faster by targeting the "general market." But the most enduring brands are squarely focused on a particular segment of the market. The most successful brands deliberately cultivate a narrow line. They know that depth is a much more effective strategy than breadth. This is particularly true for professional service firms, whose product is their intellectual capital.

Imagine a sculptor not willing to risk chipping away enough of the marble to reveal the fine detail of what makes a beautiful human form. This is similar to the behavior of companies not willing to risk a clearly defined strategy. They're afraid to keep chipping away at the generalities of their business strategy until they get to something concrete and specific. This is because they perceive "general" to be less risky than "specific." But just as no art collector is going to buy a vague sculpture, no smart customer is going to buy a vague brand.

A "general market" appeal is no appeal at all. As Eric Ryan, the co-founder of Method, manufacturer of home-care products, believes, "Consumers will pay a premium for what's scarce, and being scarce is about being different."[1]

The fact is that defining your firm's positioning strategy is usually very counterintuitive. It requires a new mental map of what truly succeeds as a business strategy. The "more is better" model that most of us carry around in our heads is the wrong mental construct. What works is narrow, not broad.

Changing your thought patterns about "narrow versus broad" is essential to defining and implementing a successful positioning strategy. That's because paradigms drive practices. You're likely to continue to respond to business challenges in the same old ways with the same old answers until you actually change how you view the issue of focus.

It wasn't until physicians became convinced of germ theory that they started finding ways to create sterile environments. First, they had to change their paradigm about what caused infections (until Joseph Lister came along, infections were thought to be caused by stale air); then they couldn't help but change their practices. Physicians starting washing their hands and cleaning their instruments.

As physician and educator Chip Souba observed, "Our mental models are not so much views and beliefs that we hold tightly as they are views and beliefs that tightly hold us."[2] Change your thinking, change your behaviors, change your results.

HOW DIFFERENTIATED ARE WE?

To gauge the current level of differentiation in your firm, rate your firm on a scale of 1 to 10, where 1 means "strongly disagree" and 10 means "strongly agree."

1. We have answered the question, "What business are we in?"

2. We have identified what we do well—our strengths and core competencies.

3. We have a clear definition of our best customer.

4. We target a specific segment of the market, not the center of the market.

5. We try to focus on what we do best instead of attempting to offer every possible feature, product, or service.

6. We avoid the promises of "complete," "full line," "wide range," or "full service."

7. We are as concerned with making our brand different as we are with making it better.

8. We avoid extending our brand name to other products and services that don't represent the core of our business.

9. We believe in the strategic advantages of "narrow and deep" over "broad and shallow."

10. We avoid imitating the marketing and claims of our competitors.

VERTICAL SUCCESS VERSUS HORIZONTAL SUCCESS

The Economist and *Wired* magazine editor Chris Anderson argues effectively that in a digitally connected world, the opportunity for most businesses is not in the "head" of the product curve, but rather the "tail." The head of the curve is where the "hits" occur—the blockbuster movies, books, and music. This is traditionally where a lot of companies have made a lot of money. Problem is, in a world of virtually unlimited choice (via the Internet), there are fewer and fewer hits; so many fewer that there is now as much (or more) money being made in the tail of the curve—the niche movies, books, and music—as in the head.

This means that the definition of a "category" is getting more and more refined. In the world of the long tail, brands shouldn't be as concerned with how they compare in their entire genre as just in their subgenre. In fact, if you've done a good job of narrowing your focus, you will have created a category of one. Creating a new category is one of the primary goals of positioning.

You don't have to be a big player in the horizontal market (the head) to be an important factor in the vertical market (the tail). Actually, vertical success is more sustainable in a world of almost unlimited choice. Better to be a big fish in a small pond (where you won't get eaten) than a small fish in a big pond (where you will).

Most companies have the unrealistic aspiration to compete across all segments of the market. But success doesn't require you to serve all segments. It just requires that you serve one *well*. This is the difference between horizontal success and vertical success. Very few companies are able to achieve real horizontal success, although many attempt it because it has the illusion of being the richest strategy. And even those horizontal players struggle mightily to earn a profit. Take General Motors—a horizontal player if there ever was one—versus Porsche, a car company that focuses on one vertical segment of the market. For most of the past decade, GM was the least profitable car company in the world. Guess who was the most profitable?

Consider the massive energy and resources required to maintain a horizontal positioning strategy, even in a relatively small industry. It only stands to reason that a vertical positioning strategy allows you to make a better product, offer better service, and potentially charge a higher price. This is why the premium brands in categories from golf clubs to outdoor furniture are niche players, not conglomerates. The very definition of excellence is to be good at something in particular. It's not only impractical for a company to be excellent at everything, it's quite impossible.

Japan has quietly produced a host of companies that demonstrate how a narrow focus can result in broad business success. Shimano earns close to $2 billion a year manufacturing close to three-quarters of the world's bicycle gears and brakes. YKK makes about half of the zip fasteners in the world. Around 75 percent of the motors for computer hard drives are made by a firm called Nidec. A Japanese company named Murata has 40 percent of the global market for the capacitors used in mobile phones and computers. Even more impressive is the fact that their margins are around 50 percent. The Japanese even have a name for these kinds of companies: *chuken kigyo*, which means strong, medium-sized firms.[3]

In the world of professional services, category knowledge is emerging as one of the leading criteria used by client companies to select firms. In a recent study among leading marketers, "actual knowledge of the industry, understanding our business" ranked first in a list of most important criteria at the credentials stage of selecting a new advertising agency.[4] A study by consultancy Reardon Smith Whittaker reports that "having an understanding of their marketplace" is the most important criteria for selecting an agency.[5] Another consultancy, Mirren, reports that the top reason agencies lose in new business competitions is "lack of relevant experience."[6] A study by the consultancy Bain and the Interactive Advertising Bureau (IAB) reported that "deep knowledge of the marketer and their industry" was the most important factor in selecting a digital marketing partner.[7]

Marketing firms that have developed deep expertise in a category therefore have a much higher success rate when it comes to business development. They're often hired without the formal "review process" involving RFPs, short lists, speculative assignments, and final presentations. When the shopping network QVC was in the market for an outside marketing partner, retail specialist Zimmerman was hired without a review.[8] That's typical for firms that know the category as well as—or better than—their clients.

THE STRATEGIC VALUE OF GOING DEEP

If you were a homesteader trying to find water, would you be more likely to find it by digging shallow holes in a lot of places or deep holes in just a few places? Differentiation is about deep versus wide. And the deeper you go, the harder it is for competitors to follow. They'll have to dig a long time to catch you, and chances are they're too busy digging lots of shallow holes anyway.

The analogy of a boat's keel works well here, too. A shallow keel might provide more speed, but a deep keel provides more stability.

Even a cooking example is appropriate to this discussion. Imagine that you're engaged in the holiday tradition of making sugar cookies. With a given amount of cookie dough, you're assigned the task of maximizing the number of both star-shaped as well as tree-shaped cookies. Of course this is quite impossible, as maximizing the number of one type of cookie means minimizing the other type. There is no way to simultaneously maximize two things. A two-pronged strategy is not a strategy. An effective value proposition maximizes something, but not everything.

The effects on your business of committing to a focus that makes the most of your strengths can be not just incremental, but exponential. A new positioning may take time to get established. In some cases, it even means your firm might have to be willing to "shrink to grow" by exercising much more careful client selection. But inevitably you will hit a "tipping point" where your investment in the new strategy will have a multiplying effect. It's very similar to the growth pattern often seen in the digital world, sometimes referred to as the "network effect." This term originally was used to describe the rapid growth of telephones in the first half of the 20th century. In the 21st century online world, this phenomenon is seen in the initial slow growth, then rapid explosion, of brands like LinkedIn and Facebook. It took LinkedIn 16 months to reach its first million users. The second million came in 11 days. Facebook took five years to attract its first 150 million users. It then doubled that number in just eight months.[9] The same kind of exponential success can occur in your firm.

Next we look at how your firm can take a deep dive to develop a differentiating value proposition.

5

Positioning as the Centerpiece of Business Strategy

A s a brand, would you rather be moderately appealing to a large group of prospects, or intensely appealing to a select group of prospects? Most businesspeople would say the latter. But most often, their business strategy centers on the former.

In life and in business, our natural tendency is to go broad instead of narrow, to want the most and the biggest. Diversification feels safer and smarter.

The problem is that if your approach is to "keep your options open" and "not limit yourself," then you actually don't have a strategy. By definition, having a strategy means deciding to do one thing but not another. By deciding to have low prices and broad selection, Wal-Mart is making a conscious decision *not* to have a high degree of sales help and ambiance. Given finite resources, Wal-Mart can't deliver low prices *and* high service. Deciding what you'll do at the expense of something else is the very essence of strategy.

Wal-Mart, like other very successful businesses, actually *wants* to be "pigeonholed." So does Southwest Airlines, which doesn't attempt to fly to every destination, offer every class of service, and fly every kind of aircraft. Rather, it actively seeks to "limit" itself to being the leading domestic low-price carrier. By flying only the Boeing 737 to only America's least-congested airports, Southwest has turned in twenty straight years of profitability.

At any given time, McDonald's has close to 60 items on its menu board. By contrast, In-n-Out Burger has mainly four menu items: hamburgers, fries, shakes, and drinks. By doing a few things extremely well, In-n-Out Burger earns a much higher profit margin than McDonalds, which must devote massive resources to inventory to deliver such variety. This is why in developed economies, focused, independent companies outperform diversified conglomerates on all key financial dimensions.[1]

It's instructive to observe how every trend toward diversification is followed quickly by a trend to refocus on core competencies. The question isn't whether diversification is a smart business strategy (it clearly isn't), but rather when business leaders will learn that trying to be good at everything usually results in being good at nothing.

Bain & Company's Chris Zook has studied the principle of focus extensively. A two-year study he led at Bain concluded that "narrower focus and concentration of resources on a single core business . . . proved the most frequent road to sustained, profitable growth."[2]

Especially in service businesses, success means determining the areas in which you intend to be excellent and where you intend to be less-than-excellent. (Just the phrase "less-than-excellent" bothers most professionals who somehow believe that it's possible to be excellent in everything). Harvard's Frances Frei tells managers that they are choosing between excellence paired with inferior performance on one hand and *mediocrity across all dimensions* on the other.[3]

The concept of branding and positioning is understood more readily in the context of consumer products, but all of the same principles apply to professional firms. This chapter examines the importance of defining what it is your firm is really selling.

WHAT ARE YOU REALLY SELLING?

While the names have been changed to protect the innocent, the following email highlights the dilemma facing many professional knowledge firms:

> My name is Kevin Calder. I work for an advertising agency called Jones & Smith. I'm hoping that you'll be able to help me crack a problem that's been nagging at me for the last two years: How to help my agency define itself.
>
> I'm writing to you at roughly 10 p.m., when the only other guy walking the floor is Otis, our janitor. I don't own this agency and I'm not the VP hoping to raise enough money to buy it. My agenda is a lot more simple: I'm just sick and tired of being sick and tired.
>
> After going through roughly two years of consistently failing to win new business, I've been asked to come up with a plan for pitching new accounts. I'm supposed to then hand this over to our CEO and his partners.
>
> Together this group will take whatever idea I come up with and debate it, beat it to death, water it down, and continue to lose new business pitches. Because they don't just need a new business plan, they need to decide what it is that they're trying to sell.

Defining what you're really selling is the essence of the value proposition. The answer is not nearly as obvious as it seems. Theodore Levitt, known for his work in marketing theory, taught his students that "nobody buys a 3/4-inch drill. They buy the expectation of a 3/4-inch hole."[4]

BECOMING HARD TO IMITATE

Business school professors David Collins and Cynthia Montgomery argue that superior performance depends on what they call "competitively valuable resources." The first test of such a resource is that it is hard to copy. Inimitability is at the heart of value creation because it limits competition. If a resource is inimitable, then the profit stream it produces is more likely to be sustainable.[5] In other words, when it comes to value creation, points of differentiation are your most important strategic assets.

Unfortunately, most value propositions are based not on inimitable points of difference, but on easily copied points of parity. This is because the leaders of the business simply haven't devoted the time and attention necessary to understand how their brand creates value. They simply assume that trying hard and "being your best" are the keys to success.

The English economist David Ricardo is credited with saying, "Profits are not made by differential cleverness, but by differential stupidity." What he meant was that most business executives simply don't make the effort to think through what actually may be obvious differences in their business model and value proposition. Peter Drucker said that well-defined value propositions work "not because they are clever, but because most institutions do not think. Anyone who asks the question, 'What does the customer really buy?' will win the race. In fact, it is not even a race since nobody else is running."[6]

The other reason most value propositions are undistinguished is because of unwillingness to sacrifice. "The essence of positioning," said advertising great Bill Bernbach, "is sacrifice." In other words, the most difficult part of strategy is deciding what you're *not*. Bernbach went on to say, "If you stand for something, you will always find some people for you and some against you. If you stand for nothing, you will find nobody against you, and nobody for you."

Because most businesses would rather be liked than disliked, loved instead of hated, they are extremely reluctant to say or do anything that would cause anybody not to like them. But of course the very nature of a positioning strategy is that your firm is right for some people but not all people. Successful brands are able to plot their position on the spectrum of love and hate. To be on either side of the spectrum is desirable; to be in the middle is death.

Brand experience expert Kathy Sierra observes, "You don't really have passionate users until someone starts accusing them of 'drinking the Kool-Aid.' Where there is passion, there is *always* anti-passion . . . or rather *passion in the hate dimension*. If you create passionate users, you have to *expect* passionate detractors. You should welcome their appearance. It means you've arrived. Forget the *tipping* point—if you want to measure passion, look for the *Kool-Aid* point."[7]

Said another way, the brands with the strongest supporters also have the strongest opponents: Microsoft, the *New York Times*, the Red Sox. This means you should stop worrying about being *pleasing* and start worrying about being *polarizing*—not necessarily in a negative way, but in a way that clearly sends the signal "we're not for everyone."

Most companies—particularly in professional services—desperately want to be loved. They don't like the idea of admirers and detractors, so they don't want to take a stand. What they don't understand is that *being lovable doesn't get you loved*. What gets you loved is standing for something.

A small business in Los Angeles, Galco's Soda Pop Stop, is the ultimate soda lover's destination. More than 500 hard-to-find soda pops are on display, carefully sourced by owner John Nese. Despite repeated overtures from PepsiCo, Mr. Nese has politely refused to carry the common and ubiquitous Pepsi brand. He knows that by standing for something (unique sodas) instead of standing for everything (all sodas), he will gain and keep his very loyal following. If you've done a thorough job of differentiation, your brand is defined by the features or customers you *don't* have.

TWO CRITICAL DIMENSIONS OF AN EFFECTIVE VALUE PROPOSITION

A value proposition exists at the crossroads of relevance and differentiation (see Figure 5.1). Relevance is about maximizing the perceived fit between your brand and your customers' needs. Differentiation is about maximizing the perceived difference between your brand and competitive brands.

Quadrant 4 in Figure 5.1 is obviously the least desirable place to be. These are the worst brands in the category; they rank low in functionality or quality and are not distinguished from competitive offerings by anything other than price.

Quadrant 1 on this matrix is the world of brands that actually do a reasonable job of meeting customer expectations in terms of features and functionality, but they are not at all differentiated from their competitors. These are the "also-rans," one of many brands that compete in typically crowded categories with a lot of pricing pressure. This is where most brands live.

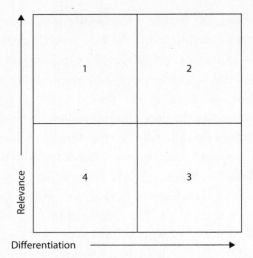

Figure 5.1 Which Quadrant Would You Prefer to Occupy?

Quadrant 3 contains the brands that are different for the sake of being different, with not enough attention paid to whether the customer really wants that feature, benefit, or option. The consumer electronics category is filled with Quadrant 3 brands.

Quadrant 2 brands have succeeded at both relevance and differentiation. While these brands may not always be the sales volume or market share leaders, they are almost always the most profitable brands in the category. They offer features and services that are highly relevant to their target prospect, and they seek to differentiate their firms in as many ways as possible.

The quest for relevance must come first. You can't differentiate your brand until you first maximize its relevance to your customers. Otherwise, you'll be lost in Quadrant 3.

The term "disruptive innovation" gets tossed about by business types who don't really understand what it means. For the most part, disruptive innovation is not about creating something out of nothing; it's usually not about a completely new technology. Rather, it's about a disruptive recombination of existing technologies and competencies. Southwest Airlines didn't reinvent air travel—the airline just packaged it up in a way that made it easier and more affordable for average Americans. Charles Schwab didn't recreate the financial system. As the world's first discount brokerage, it just used existing technologies to enable consumers to invest in faster, more efficient, and less expensive ways. Similarly, professional knowledge firms don't necessarily have to invent completely new categories of products and services as the basis of a positioning strategy; they just have to think creatively about how to recombine and repackage them in ways that have never been done before.

A CATEGORY OF ONE

Defining a positioning that's strong enough to create a new category is labeled "blue ocean strategy" by authors W. Chan Kim and Renee Mauborgne, who have identified a series of positive patterns that correlate with companies that have left the "red ocean" (red with the blood of competitors fighting over the same scraps in the same market) and instead created new opportunities in the uncharted waters of the blue ocean:[8]

- The creation of blue oceans is a key catalyst in setting an industry on an upward growth and profit trajectory.
- Blue oceans are created by both industry incumbents and startups, challenging the assumption that new entrants have advantages over established firms in creating new market space. In fact, the blue oceans created by incumbents are usually within their own core business.
- Blue oceans have created profitable growth for every company that has launched them, new and established companies alike.
- Creating a blue ocean does more than enhance profitability; it strongly enhances the standing and reputation of the brand in the customer's mind.

Apple created a blue ocean with the introduction of the iPod and iTunes. Instead of attempting to compete in the already-existing red ocean of MP3 players, Apple created a new category with an online music service that now dominates the music industry. The strategy wasn't to just be different, but to even look different. Apple made the color of the earphones and cord of the iPod the opposite of the rest of the industry: white. The ultimate value proposition puts you in a category where you're the one and only player. Eventually other brands may come along and try to imitate what you've done, but being first in the category creates a powerful competitive advantage that is exceptionally difficult for competitors to overcome. Think HP in laser printers, Microsoft in computer operating systems, Starbucks in premium coffee, and Southwest in low-cost air travel.

A BRAND IS THE CUSTOMER'S IDEA OF THE PRODUCT

One of the many definitions of a brand is that it is the customer's *idea* of your product, service, or company (versus the product, service, or company itself). A brand can't stand for two things at once. It cannot be both high end and low end, both futuristic and traditional, or both zany and business-like. Yet many companies attempt to make their brands stand for two things at once or, worse, two opposing ideas at once.

This is of course what happens in the land of line extensions, where a premium parent brand launches a lower priced version of itself. This is always a mistake, because a brand either occupies the "premium priced" spot in the customer's brain, or it occupies the "value priced" spot—but it cannot occupy both.

Countless service companies and professional service organizations attempt to deliver high-value customized services alongside low-value commoditized services. From a branding point of view, this is a strategy that not only cannibalizes the brand, but marginalizes its reputation.

If you offer a service that looks and feels undifferentiated, choose from one of these three options:

1. Add value to the commoditized service and charge more than other agencies.
2. Find a more efficient way to deliver the service and charge less than other agencies.
3. Stop doing it.

The only wrong choice is to continue to offer an average service at an average price. You must move one way or the other along the pricing continuum. This may sound more like an argument for a packaged goods brand than an agency brand, but you need either a high-cost strategy or a low-cost strategy, because an equal cost strategy is no strategy at all.

The Option of a Second Brand

When major brands face a situation where low-cost competitors are stealing share, smart companies don't try to fight low-cost competition head on; instead they develop a second brand—a "fighter brand." This allows the original brand to retain its customer base and its premium price.

To protect the Budweiser beer brand, the lower priced Busch brand was launched. To protect Pampers, P&G launched Luvs. To protect the Pentium chip's premium price, Intel introduced the lower price, lower performance Celeron chip. 3M protected the flagship Post-It brand with the "fighter" Highland brand.[9]

This strategy is perfectly suitable for professional service firms. It's what the international advertising agency Ogilvy & Mather did by developing "Redworks," a separately branded unit that exists to produce and execute the work of the higher value, higher price Ogilvy brand. Because a brand is the customer's idea of a product or service, there's really no way the brand called "Ogilvy" can stand for both high-value ideation and low-value execution.

Unfortunately, countless advertising agencies and other professional firms are attempting to make their brands stand for two very different things. In fact, they're operating two brands whether they know it or not.

Specialized knowledge and skills	Widely available knowledge and skills
Customized work	Systematized work
Approach tailored to each situation	Repeatable process with predictable outcomes
Premium pricing	Moderate to low pricing
Sells effectiveness	Sells efficiency

A brand—your firm—can choose one strategy or the other; you just can't choose both. Executing two different strategies effectively requires two separate brands.

NATURAL OUTCOMES OF A POWERFUL VALUE PROPOSITION

A strong value proposition is attractive to customers and unattractive to competitors. The idea is to claim a position that your competitors will ignore, because they either are unable to deliver the same value proposition, are uninterested in delivering it, or are unconvinced that a focused value proposition is necessary in the first place.

If you succeed, the outcomes of a successful positioning strategy will produce positive answers to all of the following statements:

- We are distinguished by a set of unique products, services, and capabilities.
- We have developed proprietary approaches that support our positioning and add value to the firm's brand.
- We are focused on what we do best and have found strategic alliances for the rest.
- Our people have a clear understanding of our positioning strategy.
- We have identified clear hiring standards for the kind of people we need to reinforce our brand.
- Our corporate identity and promotional materials reflect our positioning.
- We have a clear set of criteria for identifying prospective clients based on our positioning.
- Our positioning and focus allow us to create more proprietary intellectual property, which we are able to leverage with our clients and prospects.
- Because we have taken steps to create more value for our clients, we are able to also capture more value through our pricing and compensation agreements.
- We are differentiated not just by our capabilities, but by our point of view.

Next we look at a framework for how firms can engage in the actual process of defining or refining their value proposition, including ways to engage all important stakeholders along the way.

6

Building Brand Boundaries

In defining your value proposition, begin by identifying where your firm falls on your industry's value chain. To understand the changing dynamics of the value chain concept, observe what's happened to the music business. Consumers are still spending roughly the same amount of money on music, but the money isn't going to the record companies and music stores; it's going to iTunes. The money in the music business value chain is still there—it just moved.

The same is happening in other rapidly evolving industries. Companies are spending, but they're spending in new and different areas of the value chain. Instead of trying to squeeze the last bit of value from traditional sources of revenue, professional firms should be focused on finding a different spot on the chain.

Defining a value proposition capable of producing the most profit means selecting a place on the value chain where the offerings are still scarce and underdeveloped. For example, in the world of advertising agencies, the underdeveloped side of the value chain

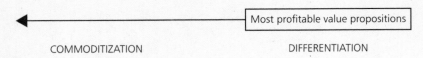

COMMODITIZATION　　　　　　　　　　　　　　DIFFERENTIATION

Figure 6.1　The Value Chain

includes such services as social media and analytics. Conversely, an advertising agency with a value proposition based around the idea of "efficient production and distribution of advertising" would be selecting a spot too far down on the value chain to have any real or perceived value in the marketplace (See Figure 6.1).

If you analyze the value propositions of most professional service firms, you'll find they are based mostly on widely available overdeveloped services; they are placing themselves on the wrong side of the value chain. By focusing on the underdeveloped features or benefits of the category, you are in effect positioning the brand not just for where the profits are, but for *where the profits will be.*

How many times have you heard business professionals rail against the idea of being "boxed in"? As the argument goes, a "box" prevents a company from doing whatever it wants and selling whatever it can to whoever might want to buy it. Exactly. No box means no strategy, no boundaries. Brands actually need a well-defined box to help define what they stand for, what they sell, and who their most likely customer is. A "boundary-less brand" is no brand at all; it's a product in search of becoming a brand.

"The essence of strategy," says Michael Porter, "is choosing what not to do."[1] No sacrifice, no strategy.

A box with four sides, in fact, defines your business strategy. You can think of these four sides as the "load-bearing walls" that represent what your organization knows and does best. Figure 6.2 illustrates a useful way to think of the four sides of the box that represent the boundaries that define the brand.

All four of these "boundaries" represent immensely important strategic questions. The answers form the basis of your positioning strategy. Let's look at each one of these boundaries individually.

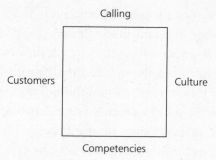

Figure 6.2 Defining Your Brand Boundaries

Calling	Why are you in business in the first place?
Customers	What types of customers or clients are you best suited to serve?
Competencies	What services or products does this type of customer need that you can best provide?
Culture	What are the formal and informal standards by which your firm makes decisions about serving its customers?

BRAND BOUNDARY I: CALLING

"Calling" might feel like a soft way to begin the process of defining a value proposition, but it's absolutely foundational to everything else. This is not about developing the usually meaningless all-purpose mission statement that hangs in aluminum frames in corporate offices across America. Thousands of companies have a mission statement, but precious few actually have a *mission*.

Without exception, the most notable companies and brands have an ambitious reason for being. This is not a coincidence. In our consulting work, we've learned that the primary unspoken question on the minds of most associates in a professional firm is: "Where is this firm headed? What are we trying to become?"

Not Just What You Are, But Why

It also has been widely documented that organizations with a sense of purpose financially outperform those whose only purpose is to generate a profit. Sure, companies are in business to make money, but that's a little like saying mothers are in the business of producing children. Mothers and businesses both have a purpose that transcends the obvious.

Peter Drucker advanced the opinion that "profit is not the purpose of a company, but rather a test of its validity." He also believed that all people and all efforts should be focused on contribution—a meaningful end result that will make an important difference for the organization.[2] This is especially true for knowledge workers, he says, who happen to be motivated by exactly the same things that motivate volunteers: a belief in the mission of the enterprise.

Knowledge Workers Are Volunteers

Consider how important purpose would be if you were leading a volunteer organization rather than a business. Purpose would be absolutely essential. Purpose is why volunteer organizations exist in the first place, and it should be why any business exists. Purpose creates not just a company of workers, but a company of believers.

Psychologist Howard Gardner goes so far as to say, "If you are not prepared to resign or be fired for what you believe in, you are not a worker, let alone a professional. You are a slave."[3]

Professionals in organizations without a defined purpose spend much of their energy wondering what it is they're supposed to be accomplishing (beyond their day-to-day tasks). Next time you're on a flight surrounded by businesspeople, one quick look around will tell you which one is associated with an organization with a motivating purpose. While most everyone else is sleeping, playing solitaire on their computer, or entertaining themselves with Sudoku, purpose-driven businesspeople are spending company time doing company business.

People in the best performing firms feel that they're part of a higher calling: to instill a sense of purpose. The creative director for a global advertising firm once said, "Give me the freedom of a tightly-defined strategy."[4] Once you know the strategy—or the purpose—you have the freedom to solve problems rather than wonder about which problems it is you're trying to solve.

Reaching for the Stars

With a stated purpose of "helping customers to create healthy, happy homes," the makers of Method soap sell a philosophy, not a product—the philosophy that cleaning products don't have to be toxic.

Jason Kilar, CEO of Hulu, the popular online video service, said Hulu was founded with the purpose "to help people find and enjoy the world's premium content how and when they want it." He acknowledges that it might not happen in his lifetime, but it's a "guiding star" that gives the organization its direction.[5] The same is true for Google's mission of cataloguing all the world's information. CEO Eric Schmidt says this will likely take 300 years.

The global electronics brand Philips has as the foundation of its value proposition "sense and simplicity"—a belief that technology should avoid technology overload and instead enable people to live simpler lives. After putting this stake in the ground, Philips moved up 12 points in InterBrand's Global Brand Scorecard survey.

When the Dove brand focused its value proposition around the purpose of fostering an understanding of "real beauty," it created one of the most successful marketing efforts in Unilever's history. "Every woman is beautiful just the way she is," says the Dove campaign. Women responded to this vision by almost doubling their purchase of Dove brand products in Unilever's largest markets around the world. Ogilvy, the agency that created the campaign, has the belief that marketers should be focused on not just "the big idea" but "the big ideal."

Purpose is not just about what your customers buy, but *what they buy into*.

Your Real Motivation

Advertising agency Crispin Porter + Bogusky credits a strong purpose with giving the agency the impetus to be great. Co-founder Alex Bogusky says early on they set out "to create the most talked about and written about advertising in the world. . . . It was embarrassingly lofty," says Bogusky, "but in the agency we shared this mission with everybody and made little cards to tape to your desk so that during the day we could make all the hundreds of decisions we were faced with, with that mission in mind."[6]

In St. Louis an advertising agency named Hughes has its offices in what's called "The Art of Living Building." In the entrance to this interesting structure is the following inscription:

> A master in the art of living draws no sharp distinction between his work and his play, his labor and his leisure, his mind and his body, his education and his recreation. He hardly knows which is which.
>
> He simply pursues his vision of excellence through whatever he is doing and leaves others to determine whether he is working or playing. To himself he always seems to be doing both.

This is about both knowing and living your calling. Because you are engaged in a purpose that transcends collecting a paycheck, you feel just as motivated at work as you do at play.

Discovering Your Calling

No company ever creates a calling. It already exists in the DNA of your firm. A calling is discovered, not created. To begin to unearth the purpose of your firm's brand, engage your management team in thinking about the following questions:

- Why does this organization exist?
- What inspires us to come to work each day?
- Besides making money, why are we in business?
- What is the meaning in what we do?
- What significant contribution do we want to make to the industry, the profession, or the world?
- What are some of our "unrealistic" expectations?
- What important problem would we like to solve?
- What would we like to create that may have never existed before?
- What would happen if our company or brand ceased to exist?
- What kind of lasting difference do we want to make?

- What do we preach?
- What are we crusading against?
- What would our enterprise be like if we were leading a movement instead of running a business?
- If our people were volunteers instead of employees, what would they be volunteering for?
- What would we want to achieve if we knew we could not fail?

This is no time for timid or "realistic" thinking. Just imagine that you're defining the ultimate stretch goal. One effective method is to ask the owners or key principals of the firm to describe the firm's "envisioned future." What would you like this firm to look like ten years from now? The answers you get to this question often contain the kernel of your firm's calling and purpose.

How to Know You've Succeeded in Defining Your Calling

A calling is about achieving a form of greatness, not bigness. It's about playing to win instead of playing not to lose. How do you know you've reached deep enough to find your calling? Here's a good test:

- **It comes from the inside; what you really believe.** Rather than being driven solely by the market, the competition, or the numbers, we have to pay attention to what drives us from inside. Your calling has to be at the center of who you really are as an enterprise. Forget about what others think and focus on what you think. You don't define your purpose through focus groups, customer opinions, or comments on your company's blog. You find it in the only place it really exists: in the soul of the company.

- **It's inspiring and motivating.** Financial goals, while important, are almost never inspiring. Yes, everyone in the firm would like to achieve a 20 percent profit so the company can give raises and pay bonuses, but there are table stakes. Professionals are not motivated primarily by money, responsibility, or even recognition, but rather by a sense of achievement.[7]

As the German philosopher Goethe observed, "If we treat people as they are, we make them worse. If we treat people as they ought to be, we help them become what they are capable of becoming."

- **It's about meaning, not money.** Again, it's not primarily about the money. There are studies that show that the things that motivate knowledge workers are the same things that motive volunteers:
  - Volunteers need a challenge.
  - They need to know the organization's mission and believe in it.
  - They need to see results.[8]
- **It's difficult—maybe impossible—to fully achieve.** Pursuing your calling is like climbing a very high mountain. Jim Collins compares it to a guiding star on the horizon, which is continually followed but never reached. In an insightful little book, *It's Not How Good You Are, It's How Good You Want to Be,* author and advertising professional Paul Arden asks the simple but potent question, "How good do you want to be?" He offers the following choices:
  - Pretty good
  - Good
  - Very good
  - The best in your region
  - The best in the world[9]

  A lot of companies throw around platitudes about being the "best," but imagine if your goal really was to be the best not just in your city, your state, or your country, but the *world.* It certainly would change a few things about how you went about your business.

The people who are most enthusiastic and contribute the most to the firm are the ones who are given big goals and big jobs. The truly outstanding brands and companies are trying not just to make money, but in some small way to change the world. "The power of purpose is not a marketing idea or a sales idea. It's a company idea," says former Procter & Gamble CMO Jim Stengel. "Purpose drives an entire organization and it answers why the brand exists."

BRAND BOUNDARY 2: CUSTOMERS

Defining a clear value proposition means having a clear definition and understanding of your customer. Think beyond *all* your customers an focus specifically on your *best* customer. For every company on the planet, there's usually a big difference between the average customer and the best customer.

It's the 80/20 rule, but taken to the extreme. Just 18 percent of Coca-Cola's customers consume 80 percent of the Coke sold. For Tide laundry detergent, 12 percent of customers account for 80 percent of the brand's total sales. But for most leading brands, an even smaller proportion of the customer base supports most of the sales volume. A meager 1 percent of the people who buy Iams pet food account for over 80 percent of the company's sales volume. It's the same for Budweiser beer. In fact, on average only 2.5 percent of customers account for 80 percent of sales of package goods brands.[10] This rule is alive and well on the Internet as well, where only 8 percent of all Internet users account for 85 percent of all clicks.[11]

The 80/20 rule—80 percent of your revenue comes from 20 percent of your customers—becomes the 95/5 rule when it comes to profits. Generally, something close to 5 percent of a company's customers generate 95 percent of its profits. Actually, because of the unprofitable customers almost every brand has, the top 20 percent of customers generate 150 percent of the profits.[12]

Applying the 80/20 rule brings great clarity to your value proposition. But ignoring the 80/20 rule can take you seriously off track. Writing specifically about companies engaged in knowledge work, business strategist Jack Bergstrand believes companies should apply and reapply the 80/20 rule over and over again. "If you keep applying the 80/20 rule to the top 20 percent, the top 1 percent ultimately creates three times more wealth than the bottom 80 percent," says Bergstrand. "Similarly, the top 20 percent creates more than 100 times the wealth of the bottom 51 percent."[13]

One Size Fits None

Failing to identify the best customer results in a "one size fits all" strategy. But the absence of a clear customer definition really means that "one size fits none." By attempting to appeal to everybody, you end up appealing to nobody.

Successful enterprises never attempt to be all things to all people, but rather *specific things to specific people.* If you are absolutely right for one customer, by definition you will be absolutely wrong for another. Says Chris Anderson in his exploration of the power of niches, "The compromises necessary to make something appeal to everyone mean that it will almost certainly not appeal perfectly to anyone—that's why they call it the *lowest common denominator.*"[14]

Gatorade achieved its remarkable success not by trying to sell to everybody who drinks liquid, but just to athletes. "Specialists in hydration for peak performance" is how the brand describes its value proposition, to which it's held true since 1967.

Who Do You Know Best?

What professional knowledge firms must do is to carefully identify their best customer; the ideal client. The way many firms define the ideal client is with subjective measures, and most firms share these criteria in common. Does this list look familiar?

- Does this client value what we do?
- Is this client easy to work with?
- Is this an innovative client willing to take some risks?
- Will this client allow us to do our best work?
- Will the client embrace us as a partner instead of a vendor?
- Do we like the people and will we enjoy working with this client?

While these criteria are important, they don't really help in proactive prospecting efforts since you can't really know the answer to any of these questions until you actually meet the client. Furthermore, none of these are *strategic* questions. Your prospects could include every kind and size of company from every kind of industry.

What's needed is a tightly defined set of objective criteria to define your best prospect. The obvious criteria would include such things as company size (revenues or employees), budget size, and geography. But even these don't go nearly far enough.

Here are seven questions that will help in defining your ideal prospect:

1. *What kinds of clients have we been most successful attracting in the past?* Review the history of your client relationships and identify the traits these companies have in common. Start with the more obvious questions of size or geography. Then apply some creative thinking to identifying common threads that might not be so obvious.

2. *What characterizes the types of assignments have we completed over the years?* This is similar to the question about characteristics of clients you've attracted in the past, only from the perspective of the nature of the assignment or engagement.

3. *Which industries or business categories do we know best?* Of the hundreds of industries identified in the Standard Industrial Code (SIC) list, which does the firm know best? In which categories have we had three or more substantial clients?

4. *What role do we play in the customer's value chain?* At what points along the client's value chain or sales funnel do we add value?

5. *What internal stakeholders do we know best?* Inside client organizations, which constituencies do we know best?

6. *What types of companies do we know best?* There are many ways to think about a "type" of company. For instance:
   - New or established
   - Products or services
   - Retailer or manufacturer
   - Upscale or average
   - Conservative or progressive
   - Entrepreneurial or traditional
   - High profile or low profile
   - Bricks and mortar or online

7. *Who are our customers' customers?* Is there a pattern in the kinds of customers our clients have? Think about age, gender, ethnicity, income, geography, and occupation.

Defining Your Positioning Strategy by the Type of Clients You Serve

The firms that have built a skill set around a particular category of business have found it much easier to compete nationally than the typical firm that tries to be all things to all people. These companies base their value proposition mainly on expertise in a particular market. In the marketing communications business, experts can be found in business-to-business, health care, pharmaceuticals, retail, entertainment, fashion, travel, real estate, building products, agriculture, financial services, natural products, retail advertising, high fashion, high technology, and even "urban marketing."

Yet another twist on this theme is expertise in a particular consumer audience. There are agencies that specialize in marketing to women, boomers, youth, Latinos, African-Americans, and outdoor enthusiasts. For advertising firms, focusing on an audience is a particularly powerful form of positioning, because it allows them to become expert in understanding the attitudes, values, habits, wants, needs, motivations, and behavior of a particular class of people. This in-depth knowledge is infinitely attractive to the prospective clients who market their products to these audiences.

The founders of an advertising firm in the competitive New York market started as generalists, only to discover that they do in fact have an area of expertise. The brands they attracted have an important thing in common: They're purchased by the affluent. The agency backs up its areas of specialization by publishing a "luxury survey" featured in *Advertising Age*.

An agency in the Midwest owns the most important demographic in the country: seniors. This agency is expert in marketing products and services purchased by the market segment with the most disposable income—a smart business strategy that has fueled impressive growth.

Higher education is the focus of a multiple-office firm that counts some of the country's largest and most prestigious universities as clients. Beyond advising these institutions on improving enrollment and admissions, this firm conducts tuition pricing elasticity studies and implements programs designed to improve development and fundraising.

Another marketing firm with historical expertise in agricultural marketing found a more compelling way to describe its core competence: it knows the "ruralpolitan" market. This means that this agency would be a good choice for clients who market not only farm equipment or pesticides, but also 4 × 4 trucks and firearms. This is a brilliant business strategy that can feed this agency's new business machine for years to come.

There are limitless creative ways to define the type of clients you know best. Here are some more not-so-obvious examples we've encountered in our consulting work:

- Companies with a triple bottom line (profit, people, planet)
- Companies that market brands recommended by a trusted advisor (such as financial services)
- Companies that market highly engineered brands (such as pharmaceuticals)
- Franchised companies
- Public eye companies (regulated companies like public utilities)
- Brands that require membership (institutions you have to join)
- Companies that take sides (organizations with a social mission)
- Companies that are under siege (in need of reinvention)
- Companies with altitude (aviation-related companies)

Firms in the process of defining a positioning strategy is the fear of "getting too narrow." But of course that's the whole point—getting narrow. The narrower your positioning strategy, the more leverage you have in the marketplace. Consider the construction of a teeter totter. The further you move the fulcrum to one side, the more leverage you produce on the other side. Your job is to move the fulcrum as far to one side as possible. As Archimedes said, "Give me a lever long enough and I can move the world."

One of my favorite examples of this principle is a marketing firm in southern California formed by executives with experience in healthcare marketing. When positioning their firm, they asked themselves a series of questions, each of which pushed the fulcrum further and further to one side:

Q: What do we know best?
A: Healthcare marketing.

Q: What aspect of healthcare marketing?
A: Pharmaceuticals.

Q: What aspect of pharmaceuticals?
A: Chronic diseases.

Q: Which chronic diseases?
A: Cancer, HIV, and diabetes.

Is this a narrow business strategy? Without question it is. But it's one with remarkable potential. Think of how many people in the world suffer from one of these three diseases. The example of this firm also debunks one of the other major resistances to positioning: "Won't we get bored with a narrow focus?" On the contrary, going deep into a chosen area of expertise allows you to explore absolutely new territory, solve new problems, and provide new thought leadership. So instead of just creating ads for drugs that treat these chronic diseases, this firm has created video games to teach diabetic kids how to use their insulin pumps, podcasts to help cancer patients deal with their disease, and webisodes to teach recently diagnosed HIV patients how to announce the news to their loved ones.

Look at which firms are doing the interesting work and breaking new ground in any field and the answer is always the specialist, not the generalist.

BRAND BOUNDARY 3: COMPETENCIES

When it comes to your firm's abilities, the task is to identify not just capabilities but *competencies*. Competencies are capabilities of the organization that can be delivered in a dependable, differentiating way.

Bain's Chris Zook, who has written extensively about the concept of what is "core" to a company, believes that a core capability is defined by 1) its ability to create economic value for a customer, and 2) its ability to provide a source of differentiation against competitors.[15] In other words, a core competence can be determined by plotting it on the axes shown in Figure 6.3.

The pioneering work in this area was done by Gary Hamel and C.K. Prahalad in their paper "The Core Competence of the Corporation" and then later in the book *Competing for the Future* in which they observed:

> Senior management can't pay equal attention to everything; there must be some sense of what activities really contribute to long-term corporate prosperity. The goal therefore is to focus senior management's attention on those competencies that lie at the center, rather than the periphery, of long-term competitive success.[16]

In other words, it's not enough to just identify the things you do well. Competitors may have similar core competencies. You must go further to find what could be considered a distinctive competence. This is often the result of disaggregating your short list of core competencies—breaking them down into component parts to find what's truly distinctive.

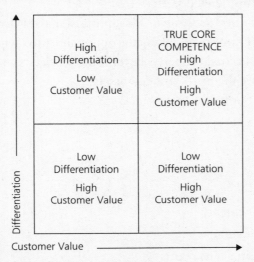

Figure 6.3 The Core Competence Quad

Getting to What's Core

In defining competencies, here are ten of the right questions to get you started:

1. *What do we do particularly well; perhaps better than most firms in our industry?* What are the areas in which we would give our organization an A grade? Where are we best in class?
2. *What's the one thing our firm is most known for?* This is essentially a complexity reduction exercise. What would the firm look like if it had only one service line? What would we do if we were starting this firm for the first time?
3. *What outcomes are our customers seeking?* Clients don't buy your capabilities; they buy the results your capabilities can produce. What are the primary outcomes your clients are seeking?
4. *What different or innovative services do we offer?* What do we do that most other firms don't do? What special offerings do we have that are exclusive to our firm?
5. *In which areas do we have specialized knowledge?* What is the unique intellectual capital we bring to client assignments? In what areas could we be considered expert?
6. *What strategic assets do we own?* Most professional service firms perform "work for hire," overlooking the opportunity to own or develop their own intellectual property. Beyond the services you provide to clients, what are the firm's strategic assets?

    Here are a few things to consider:

    - Copyrights
    - Trademarks
    - Patents
    - Licenses
    - Licensing agreements
    - Royalty agreements
    - Revenue-sharing agreements

- Databases
- Joint ventures
- Professional networks
- Domain names
- Brand names
- Strategic partnerships
- Specialized knowledge bases
- Proprietary processes
- Certifications
- Online properties
- Permission-based lists
- Source code
- Software applications

7. *How are we distinguished by the way we think?* What are the firm's philosophies and beliefs? What do we preach? What are some polarizing issues on which we have a strong opinion? Do we have a unique approach to such topics as people management, organization development, or client service?

8. *What methods and approaches do we use?* To what extent have we developed proprietary methodologies that help us create value for our clients? Do we have a unique approach to such things as workflow management, compensation, or problem solving?

9. *How are we differentiated by our organization or structure?* Does our structure or organization set us apart from other firms? Do we take a different approach to functions, disciplines, or reporting relationships?

10. *What are we not?* Saying what you are is the easy part. Saying what you are *not* is where your positioning strategy is really defined. Don't view this as a negative exercise. Consider the experience of the visitor who walked into the studio of the great Renaissance painter and sculptor Michelangelo. In the middle of his studio was a large block of marble. The visitor asked what he intended to do with it. "From that rock,"

said the great artist, "I will sculpt David." The visitor found it hard to imagine how anyone could create anything from a big square rock. He then asked the master how he was able to create a human body from a block of marble. "Oh, it's very simple," said Michelangelo. "I just take a chisel and knock off all the parts that aren't David."

That's what positioning is about. You don't start from nothing. You just remove the parts that aren't you.

Doing What You Love

Especially for new or smaller entrepreneurial companies, it's important to take into consideration not just what you *should* do, but what you *want* to do. Where does your passion want to take you? It's useful to consider your interest vs. your expertise (see Figure 6.4).

Focusing on a Core Competency

Drawing again on direct experience with marketing communications firms, let's look at some examples of positioning strategies that center on a competency. Advertising agencies offer services and disciplines ranging

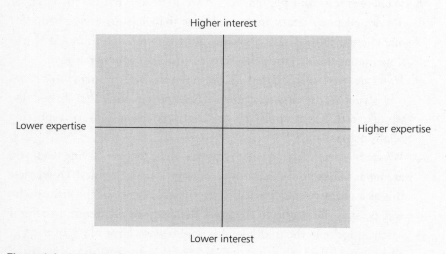

Figure 6.4   Interest vs. Expertise

from basic mass media advertising to sales promotion to events. Many of the most successful are focused exclusively on one of these disciplines, having built a reputation as a specialist with a track record and credentials that attract the Fortune 500 as clients. These firms are good examples of the "narrow is not small" phenomenon.

There are agencies devoted exclusively to such disciplines as customer relationship management, public relations, public affairs, experiential marketing, digital marketing, shopper marketing, and media placement. In fact, some of the firms that only plan and place media (vs. creating ads) are global behemoths handling accounts worth billions.

Some firms are distinguished by a very strong (and sometimes controversial) point of view, from the way they service their clients (no account executives) to the way they are paid by their clients (value pricing in place of fees or commissions). In fact, the area of compensation is one of the most visible ways some agencies are breaking from the pack, choosing approaches such as owning their intellectual property, charging for ideas instead of execution, or earning a success fee.

TWBA/Chiat/Day, best known for its decades-long work for Apple, has built a reputation based on a philosophy it calls "disruption." While other firms may talk about the concept of disruption, Chiat/Day has integrated this theme into every corner of the agency. The centerpiece is a toolbox it calls Disruption Central, containing more than 20 tools and exercises. It has Disruption Zones, Disruption Days, Disruption Workshops, and even Disruption Triggers (seven ways to identify a brand that needs some disruptive thinking).

Beyond a straightforward focus on a particular discipline, there are creative ways to package and express your experience, as some of these agencies have done:

- We build the internal brand (marketing communications directed to employees and internal stakeholders of the brand).
- We launch new products.
- We create sensory experiences (through experiential or event marketing).

- We find and cultivate the high lifetime value customers (versus just selling products).
- We match your brand with the consumers that share your values..

A positioning strategy based on a deep expertise or competency obviously works as well for other professional service firms as it does for marketing communications firms. That's why some of the most notable law firms do just corporate law, some of the most profitable accounting firms do just tax work, and some of the most in-demand architectural firms design just healthcare facilities.

BRAND BOUNDARY 4: CULTURE

The final crucial element of the value proposition is the culture of your firm; the company personality that is reflected in everything you do. Culture is a direct result of your values and principles, the standards by which your firm makes daily decisions.

Culture is like flypaper. The richer it is, the stickier the paper. Firms with a strong culture weigh every decision against a set of strongly held principles. A strong culture provides a framework for decision making and defines your firm's "rules of engagement."

A company that lacks a set of strong beliefs, values, or principles almost always also lacks a differentiating value proposition. The leading marketing trade magazine recently ran a story titled "Is There Anything You Won't Do?" exposing the frenetic, indiscriminate chase for new business by many advertising agencies that are willing to throw their principles out the window and do anything to get the account. Behavior like this not only devalues these firms, but serves to commoditize the entire category.

Strong Principles Create a Strong Culture

San Francisco-based Goodby Silverstein & Partners is an example of a firm that sticks to its guns. Years ago it published a handbook titled "How to Work Here," which states that it "exists to insure that Goodby, Silverstein

& Partners is different from any place that ever was or will be." This well-crafted summary of culture and beliefs articulates both what to expect (great parties, 25-cent beers in the Coke machine) as well as what not to expect (a slick organization, designer clothes).

Prominent on the list of "what not to expect" is "a democracy." The agency has a firmly held belief that in a creative business like advertising, not everyone in the firm has an equal say in what gets presented or produced. The leaders of the firm reserve that right. Another principle is that there is never an official "agency line," meaning they don't expect every team member to agree, even in a client meeting. To some professional firms this would be heresy. But to Goodby, it's part of what makes the firm different.

The most effective culture-defining principles are memorable, differentiating, polarizing, and more valuable than money. Let's take a closer look at each identifier.

Is it Memorable?

The reason most employees can't recite their company's values is because the values are pretty forgettable. That's because most companies simply copy the same tired language they've seen other firms use: quality, leadership, customer service. It's like wallpaper.

In companies where associates *can* recite the principles that guide the firm, it's because the principles are stated in a way that makes them hard to forget. "Nurture stupidity," says the manifesto of one firm. "Do not rush to judgment of ideas. Lunacy is an area most people fear, and therefore it remains largely unexplored." This is a pretty memorable way to state a principle.

In southern California an advertising firm memorably named David & Goliath looked inside its corporate DNA and found what it believes describes what the firm is all about: "bravery." Says founder David Angelo:

> Brave is more than a word—it's an irrefutable truth. A truth that gives you permission to believe that if you face your fears, anything is possible. Brave isn't about charging blindly down a hill wielding a huge sword—it's

about outwitting the competition, being nimble, scrappy, and relentless. So we decided to fully embrace "brave" and give it more meaning than ever before. *We started putting everything we do through a "brave" filter.*[17]

The firm then set about memorably executing its belief in "brave" by:

- Redesigning its logo to support a braver tone of the brand
- Creating stationery (your name here & Goliath) to reflect that everyone is a "David" with Goliaths to slay
- Designing military-style badges that are awarded for extreme acts of bravery
- Adding "bravery" as a criterion in the development of marketing strategies
- Establishing a brave initiation process for new hires, who have to participate in random acts of bravery
- Putting up a "Wall of Goliaths" as a lobby display, where every staff member has his or her biggest fear framed as a reminder to conquer it
- Creating a nonprofit organization called The Brave Alliance (www.bravealliance.org)

Is it Differentiating?

In workshops we have on this topic, we often perform a "mindreading" trick in which we ask the workshop participants to write on a piece of paper the three most important values in their firm. While they're writing, we turn the flipchart away from the audience and write these three words: "Honesty, Integrity, Respect." We then ask a volunteer from the audience to share his or her responses. More than 90 percent of the time, what we listed matches the respondent's list exactly.

Are these principles (honesty, integrity, respect) important? Of course they are. But aren't they really the cost of entry in business? Would you really ever knowingly work for a company that didn't have these values?

Just like other dimensions of your value proposition, the principles that define your culture must be not only relevant, but *differentiating*.

Here some other oft-quoted principles that are relevant to most firms, but don't really do anything to set the firm apart from anyone else:

- Innovation
- Balanced lifestyle
- Quality work
- Team attitude
- Keeping commitments
- Proactivity
- Mutual trust and respect
- Client orientation
- Flexibility
- Straight talk

Can You Argue Its Opposite?

Another way you can tell a culture-defining principle is if the opposite can be reasonably argued. A stated principle that everyone agrees with doesn't do much to set you apart from the crowd. "We approach our work with a team attitude." Not differentiating (and not even interesting). On the other hand, "We don't divulge our client list" is a principle you can argue either way.

Here are a few more:

- We don't believe in presenting speculative work in new business presentations.
- We respectfully decline participating in the traditional RFP process.
- We actively pursue multiple clients in the same category, believing the knowledge and expertise we gain accrues to the benefit of our clients.
- We don't believe in presenting options. We present one recommendation at a time: our best.
- We believe in putting senior people in client-facing roles, with junior people in supporting roles, not vice versa.
- We outsource everything our clients consider a "commodity."

- We believe in a work environment where our associates are free to manage their time on their own terms as long as they are delivering the expected value for our clients.
- We won't just do it your way, or our way—we'll keep working until both parties are satisfied.
- We don't do timesheets. Our pricing is determined by the value we create.

Dan Weiden, co-founder of Weiden & Kennedy in Portland, Oregon, the long-time agency for Nike and creator of "Just Do It," says, "We credit a lot of our success to building the kind of culture that both repels and attracts people."[18] Among other things, W&K is adamant about no titles for anyone—including Dan Weiden himself.

Will You Sacrifice For It?

The last part of this exercise in defining culture-defining principles is an easy one to understand: Ask yourself if you'll hold to the principle even when it costs you money. If the answer is yes, you've identified a defining principle. Frank Lloyd Wright was famous for turning down assignments where he felt his principles of "organic architecture" would be compromised. Rather than making Wright poorer, it helped make him one of the most famous architects of all time. The character Howard Roark in Ayn Rand's *The Fountainhead* (whom many believe was modeled after Mr. Wright) said it this way: "I don't build in order to have clients. I have clients in order to build!"[19]

It's one thing to state a belief and quite another to defend it when a significant amount of money is on the line. In situations like this, there's actually something much more important at stake than money: your firm's reputation and credibility. Money, once lost, is fairly easy to get back. There's always more money where that came from. But reputation, once lost, is very difficult to get back. Far too often, leaders of otherwise talented and successful firms make the mistake of putting money first. Alas, a principle is a principle only when it costs you money.

A few years ago Chicago-based Cramer-Krasselt produced and placed in the Super Bowl a well-crafted commercial for its then-client CareerBuilder

.com. When the ads failed to win the "best-liked" accolades in the next morning's issue of *USA Today*, CareerBuilder announced they would be putting its business into review.

C-K's response was to promptly resign the business. Not only was the client shocked, but the move took the entire industry by surprise, since most agencies react to situations like this by investing tremendous amounts of money and emotional energy in defending a piece of business they have little chance of retaining.

But C-K's move wasn't based on the low odds of retaining the business; it was based on the firm's sense of integrity and self-worth. It earned them the praise of industry observers worldwide. Resigning CareerBuilder enhanced the agency's reputation and is believed to be one of the factors that led to Porsche effectively handing Cramer-Krasselt its business without a review.

Controversial Cultures

One of America's fiercely independent agencies, The Richards Group in Dallas, is noted for the strongly held beliefs of its founder Stan Richards. For starters, it is the stated policy of the agency to never defend a current client who has chosen to put its account into review. The vast majority of advertising agencies would consider this a foolhardy policy (despite the fact that 80 percent of the time the client leaves the agency anyway). Among The Richards Group's other controversial beliefs and practices:

- No internal use of email (associates are encouraged to leave their offices and talk in person)
- No one gets a window office (all offices are inside an open-office environment, and the shared spaces—conference rooms, break rooms, office equipment—all get the windows)
- Clients that have contributed more than the desired profit margin of 20 percent get a refund check at the end of the year (personally delivered by Stan Richards)

Besides helping to create a strong, unique culture, these principles are effective not because they are universal (which they certainly are not) but because they are *debatable.* One could certainly argue the opposite of all of these principles.

In design circles, Toronto-based Bruce Mau has created a larger-than-life reputation not only by doing incredible design work, but because his firm Bruce Mau Design is famous for its distinctive culture. Among Mau's controversial principles:

- Make mistakes faster (try new things, fail fast, and move on)
- Don't enter award competitions (we should be judged by our success in the marketplace)
- Avoid software (using software too early in the conceptual process produces poor substitutes for real ideas)
- Don't clean your desk (surround yourself with things that inspire you)

One more example from the world of marketing is New York's Anomaly, definitely not what one would consider a typical ad agency. Co-founder Carl Johnson once made a presentation to fellow advertising professionals in which he began by saying, "In describing Anomaly, I'd like to talk to you not about our capabilities, but our beliefs." Among this firm's differentiating beliefs is their policy of always putting some "skin in the game" when it comes to client compensation agreements. Their strong preference is to own the intellectual property they develop for their clients. They never charge for their time, not only because they don't believe in it, but because they don't keep timesheets. And when one of their associates develops a good idea for a client, the firm allows the individual associate to keep some of the ownership of the idea. When Anomaly is included in a competitive review, it's an orange in a bowl of apples.

THE CONFLUENCE OF CALLING, CUSTOMERS, COMPETENCIES, AND CULTURE

Defining your firm's brand boundaries—Calling, Customers, Competencies, and Culture—is the most important form of strategic development you can engage in. Unless you answer these essential questions, most other

GETTING TO YOUR PRINCIPLES

To better understand the beliefs and principles that define your culture, look deep inside your company's genetic makeup and ask the following questions:

- What is core to the culture of the firm?
- What are the things about the company that we would never change?
- What do we fight for?
- What do we do or say that creates advocates?
- When it comes to business, what are the lines we draw in the sand?
- What are the things we will always do, and the things we will never do?

forms of strategic planning are pointless. Your firm's business strategy and tactics must revolve around a clearly defined value proposition.

Many "offsites" are only marginally useful exercises in goal setting that often avoid the central question of strategy making: What market should we serve? No professional service firm can serve all markets with all services.

The next chapter looks at how your can test your value proposition against a set of criteria that will help ensure long-term success.

CHAPTER 7

Validating Your Value Proposition

After you've taken your firm through the journey of building an effective value proposition, how do you know you've arrived at your destination? The best place to start is to make sure you've struck the right balance between authenticity and aspiration (see Figure 7.1).

A positioning that's too authentic is too focused on where the business *was* instead of where the business is going. On the other hand, a value proposition that's too aspirational is a shot in the dark based more on

Authenticity   Aspiration

Where the business has been   Where the business is going

Figure 7.1 The Balance of Authenticity and Aspiration

hopes than on abilities. The best solution isn't to draw the line right in the middle of the spectrum, but rather to err on the side of aspiration. Your value proposition must be looking even more to the future than to the past; otherwise you'll be cycling back to the reinvention process much sooner than you either want or need to.

BE ROOTED IN THE FUTURE, NOT THE PAST

If you base your value proposition only on facts, you will be defining a position for the present and the past, but not one for the future. Data can tell you only what *has* happened, not what will happen. Facts don't predict the future—only a theory predicts the future.[1]

Your value proposition must be based not on where the money is, but where the money will be. And to know where the money will be, requires that you have a well-founded theory about what will happen in your market and why.

The point is that your value proposition will not be found as much in the archive of facts about your brand, market, and category as in the storehouse of knowledge, in your company that can peer ahead and predict (see Table 7.1). This is not the equivalent of an "educated guess," but rather a well-constructed theory of the future based on an understanding of what happens to a brand, a market, or a customer under various sets of circumstances. A positioning that's grounded mostly on past performance and past customer needs will be true to what you are, but you'll miss the opportunity to define who you *wish* to be.

Table 7.1 Fact-Driven versus Theory-Driven Value Propositions

Fact-Driven Value Proposition	Theory-Driven Value Proposition
Based on an understanding of what *has* happened.	Based on what's actually happening or what's likely to happen.
Looks at facts and figures that explain the past.	Looks at circumstances that are likely to affect the future.

THE VALUE PROPOSITION TEAM

While the leadership for developing a strong value proposition must come from the top, it will take the energy and ingenuity of several key people in your organization to maximize the effectiveness of this process. In selecting this group, look for individuals who would score well in the five areas shown in Table 7.2.

Equally important are selection criteria you should *not* use. Selecting members based on political expediency is usually a mistake. Even if you have officers, department heads, or others who feel they merit membership on a strategic planning team, unless they meet the criteria in Table 7.2 it will prove more a hindrance than a help to include them. Simply explain that you are assembling a special team that exists outside of the agency's normal organizational structure, and that you are purposefully selecting people who may or may not be part of an already-existing management team or committee.

Remember that the purpose of this group is to evaluate and generate ideas and recommendations, not necessarily to make decisions. All decisions about which ideas to adopt and execute will be left to the leaders of the enterprise. This is about co-creation, not consensus. Strategy making requires the creative thinking of a number of individuals, but it's ultimately not a completely democratic process.

Table 7.2   Essential Qualities of the Value Proposition Team

Strategic thinking	Are the people good creative thinkers who can bring new viewpoints to the conversation and help us rethink our assumptions?
Collaboration	Are the people good at listening and building on others' thinking? Are they good on their feet in a group setting?
Respect	Are the people generally respected within the firm? Are they credible to their colleagues?
Proactivity	Do the people have a proactive (rather than reactive) work style? Are they in the habit of offering up ideas without waiting to be asked?
Business acumen	Do the people understand what drives the firm's success? Do they understand basic organizational and operational issues of the business?

Individual Minds, Not Hivemind

As is true with other elements of your value proposition, don't get hung up on the words. The phrasing can come later. Define the *substance* first, style later. Countless management groups get lost in a debate over "how to say it" rather than devoting energy to "what to say."

It's also important not to count on traditional "brainstorming" techniques to produce these ideas. Surprisingly, brainstorming in a group usually produces fewer ideas than asking each individual on the team to think and work independently. The technique we employ in our workshops is to ask each participant to think about these questions in advance of a group session.

The advertising business has a discipline referred to as "brand planning" or "account planning," which is devoted to uncovering consumer insights in unconventional ways. One of the tenets of brand planning is that traditional focus groups are almost always a poor way of learning what people really think. As one dramatic example, close to 90 percent of all new products fail despite their endorsement by focus groups.

Some of the innovative techniques used by brand planners in the quest to generate ideas or insights about a brand are shown in the list below.

Mood pictures	Respondents are asked to associate different brands with different pictures representing moods such as fear, pride, or risk.
Debate team	Dividing the group into opposing sides and letting them debate for and against the brand.
Obituaries	The brand has died. What from, who is sad, who will come to the funeral?
Opposites	What if the brand became its opposite?
Brand party	Describe the brands that come to a party.
Deprivation	What if you couldn't use the brand?
"Brandicide"	What methods would you use to kill the brand?
Outsiders	Imagine that strong brands from other categories enter our category.

Front page article	Write the future of the brand.
Psychiatrist's couch	The brand visits the psychiatrist to talk about its problems.
Brand role play	What if the brand was a car, animal, country, celebrity, or store?
Screenplay	Write a compelling screenplay for the brand.
Moments of truth	What are the key decision points in the customer's decision to buy the brand?

This isn't to say there isn't a time and place to bring your entire strategic planning group together in the same room to evaluate options; just don't count on a group setting to generate your best ideas.

Creative consultant Tom Monahan teaches ideation techniques, one of which he calls "100 MPH Thinking," an approach in which your team generates a lot of ideas in a short amount of time. With this very effective technique, instead of carefully deliberating about each dimension of your positioning strategy, your goal is a lot of ideas, quickly. This is an exercise focusing on quantity without regard to quality. By generating a large quantity of ideas, you'll actually increase your chances of also producing some quality ideas. In Monahan's experience, the first 70 percent of the ideas you generate will be only so-so—the obvious ideas. But the last 30 percent are more likely to be gems, or at least diamonds in the rough.

Instead of applying the psychological pressure of "OK, let's come up with fifteen good ideas," you instead engage in the fast idea generation that sometimes is called "rapid creative prototyping," which may result in fourteen mediocre ideas, but one *great* one. The practice of rapid idea generation is built on the premise that it takes quantity to get to quality. Another reason it's so effective is that it shuts down idea-smothering judgment. Judgment stops ideas dead in their tracks. When judgment is applied to a bad idea, the team loses its morale and momentum. When judgment is applied to a good idea, the team stops ideating. So judgment during the early phases of creative thinking throws things off track either way.

Another benefit: Rapid idea generation builds failure into the process. It acknowledges that, as Monahan says, "The best scientists fail more than the average scientists. The best films have miles of outtakes on the editing room floor."[2]

An Hourglass Approach

Expect to follow what could be considered an "hourglass" process, where you begin the initial ideation process with a larger group. The process then narrows at the point where the principals or owners of the firm must take the input and ideation and make a decision about the positioning strategy (remember, this is about co-creation but not necessarily consensus). The process then broadens again at the point where you're ready to execute your positioning strategy, because you'll need teams of your best people to bring your practices in line with your positioning.

ASKING THE RIGHT QUESTIONS

To ensure that you have arrived at a truly differentiating value proposition, you must subject it to a series of tough questions designed to test its validity and effectiveness. Engage your team in an honest evaluation of eight areas:

1. *Does your value proposition feel authentic?*

    Your business strategy should make you stretch, but it should feel invigorating, not frustrating. It should build on your natural strengths, not strengths you only wish you had.

2. *Does it make your company intensely appealing?*

    A strong yet narrow focus makes your brand very attractive to a very specific target customer. Remember, the goal is to be intensely appealing to *someone* instead of mildly appealing to *everyone*.

3. *Does it have strong barriers to entry?*

    A tight definition of your positioning means that you've created strong boundaries that make it difficult for competitors to enter your new category.

4. *Is it hard to find an exact substitute?*

Customers and clients will find it difficult or impossible to identify another brand that delivers the features and benefits you offer.

5. *Does it result in fewer competitors?*

A narrow focus, by definition, means you'll have fewer direct competitors than broadly defined brands. In fact, the stronger the value proposition, the more likely it is that there won't be *any* other brands like yours in the marketplace.

6. *Can you charge higher prices?*

Since the very point of a strong value proposition is to compete on the basis of differentiation instead of low cost, an effective value proposition should allow to you maintain premium pricing for your brand.

7. *Does it make your sales cycle shorter and less expensive?*

One of the signs of a well-defined strategy is that it reduces your cost of making a sale. In professional services, well-positioned firms often are hired without a competitive review and are asked to do less work to prove their ability to do the job. This means fewer lengthy RFP responses or speculative work presentations.

8. *Have you created a new category?*

A truly relevant and differentiating value proposition creates a business category that has never existed before, rather than trying to compete in existing categories. It puts you in the uncharted waters of the "blue ocean" instead of slugging it out with direct competitors in the bloodied "red ocean."

The Story of Your Brand

Much has been written about the power of storytelling, even in the context of leading and managing a business. Consider your positioning strategy as the story of how and why your company came to be, what it loves to do, what it cares about, and how it thrives against competitors.

Writing in the thought-provoking book *Baked In*, marketing professionals Alex Bogusky and John Winsor argue that an effective brand story helps bring together all the different elements of your firm's strategy in a way that energizes people and attracts prospects.[3]

Of course the problem most brands have—including most professional firms—is that they don't really have a differentiating brand story. So they rely on some form of marketing—the website, the company brochure—to make one up anyway. These invented stories are almost universally weak and uninteresting (something along the lines of "full service," "focus on quality," and "excellence in client service") because they're not based on any kind of unique value proposition. Bogusky and Winsor suggest that there are four variations of this situation:

1. *The product has no story and neither does the marketing.* This is the firm that has both failed to build its brand boundaries and failed to develop any kind of interesting marketing program.

2. *The product has no story, but the marketing makes one up anyway.* This describes most professional service firms, which end up with mostly a generic description of who they are and what they do.

3. *The product has a story, but the marketing tells a different one.* In this case, the firm does in fact have a differentiating value proposition but has failed to convey it in its self-promotion for fear of "leaving someone or something out."

4. *The product has a story, and the marketing tells it well.* This is the firm with a compelling value proposition and a marketing approach that amplifies it.

Strong brands have a strong narrative—an interesting answer to the request, "Tell me about your firm."

As novelists know, good stories almost always include an element of conflict—an antagonist of some kind. This is why your brand story must articulate not just what you're for, but what you're *against*. Not just who you are, but who you are *not*. Not just what you do, but what you *don't* do, and why.

The next chapter looks at how to bring this story to life.

CHAPTER 8

Without Execution, There Is No Strategy

Back in 1943 General Motors invited a talented young management consultant named Peter Drucker to study the company from the inside out. The book that ultimately was produced as a result of this assignment influenced management thinking for decades to come. But Drucker's recommendations were largely ignored by GM itself, which as the largest carmaker in the world remained stubbornly bureaucratic and complacent.[1]

Brilliant strategies are only brilliant if they are executed. Your value proposition must not only say, it must *be*.

"Operationalizing" a positioning strategy means bringing it to life in all of your firm's major business practices. This involves identifying key imperatives that will need to be addressed with the same commitment and urgency as client business. Unless you translate your initiatives into action, they are really only intentions. And the only way these initiatives will get done is if the top management of the firm models the behavior it expects of other associates. Commitment, discipline, and action start from the top.

If it's important to the CEO and the management team, it will be important to everyone else.

Most important, if the firm's leaders have high expectations, they will get high performance. If they have low expectations, the status quo will prevail. In fact, research has shown that High expectations centered on a goal that takes unusual effort produces unusual results. Normal expectations centered around a goal that takes the *usual* effort produces the *usual* results.

Leaders and managers can't delegate their responsibility for personal involvement in executing the firm's positioning strategy. "Many people regard execution as detail work that's beneath the dignity of a business leader," observe Larry Bossidy and Ram Charan in *Execution*. "To the contrary, it's a leader's most important job."[2] A leader's ultimate success isn't a result of strategy, but *execution*. Nobody has ever achieved greatness without results.

Executing your positioning strategy isn't just an important thing; it's the *only* thing. Unless you actually put your strategy into action, nothing will have been accomplished. Without execution, there is no strategy. And if you really analyze the business landscape, you'll realize that the main difference between mediocre firms and great ones is not just vision, but execution.

The problem is most firms are too busy working on yesterday's problems to work on today's strategic imperatives. In Chapter 7, this was defined as backward-looking and lacking aspiration. This chronic challenge can produce real cynicism among employees of professional knowledge firms. They begin to doubt not necessarily the sincerity of management, but rather the degree to which management is really committed.

Chapter 6 focused on defining the boundaries of your brand by examining your Calling, Customers, Competencies, and Culture. Now you must engage your management team in bringing your positioning strategy to life in five key areas: Services, Staffing, Self-promotion, Systems, and Staging. This chapter will cover each of these five S's.

- The area of *services* is about refining and redefining the capabilities needed to support the positioning strategy. It's about not just client deliverables, but more important, client outcomes. This includes a definition of practice areas, client selection, cross-functional collaboration, client service approaches, and the development of unique intellectual capital to support your value proposition.

- The area of *staffing* is about recruiting, hiring, and developing the talent necessary to bring your positioning to life, including performance planning, professional development, information sharing, internal communication, talent management, and career development.
- The area of *self-promotion* is about marketing and promotion your own brand, including prospecting, new business development, publicity, and online reputation management.
- The area of *systems* is about your firm's approach to getting things done, including project management capabilities and practices, workflow process, resource allocation, pricing, and scope management.
- The area of *staging* is about your physical and virtual place of business, including first impressions, the working environment, equipment and resources, technological capabilities, and maximizing all the brand touch points of the firm.

Executing your positioning strategy means making deliberate decisions about what to do more of and what to do less of; what to start doing and what to stop doing. Let's look at how to do this in each of these areas. Additional ideas for differentiating your firm's brand are listed in Appendix B.

SERVICES

To make sure your service line-up supports your positioning strategy, ask the questions discussed below.

New or Special Capabilities

To fully deliver on our value proposition, what is lacking from our mix of services and capabilities?

When you have a clear view of the value you want to create for your clients—in other words, a positioning—it provides a clear blueprint for your line-up of products, services, and capabilities. Juice, a New York-based marketing firm specializing in pharmaceuticals, offers not just advertising services, but an entire go-to-market platform for introducing new products to healthcare professionals.

Outmoded Services

What should we stop doing?

With a defined positioning in hand, it's equally important to identify the services that should be discontinued or de-emphasized. This includes not only the services that have simply outlived their usefulness, but also those that simply don't fit (or worse, contradict) the value proposition you've defined for your firm.

This is exceptionally difficult for most firms, because the natural tendency is to think "the more services, the more business." Just remember, "full service" is not a strategy.

A law firm with a renewed focus on real estate law must give up its tax practice. Your brand can stand for something, but it can't stand for everything.

Business Partnerships

For the needed services we don't or can't offer, what are our options for business partnerships or outsourcing?

Sometimes your focus will call for ancillary services that your firm will need to provide via a supplier or partner. This can be for several reasons:

- The service is needed so infrequently that it's economically infeasible to staff for it.
- The service is so specialized that it's better done by a business partner with capabilities you don't have.

- The service is so "commoditized" that your clients will not be willing to pay anything but an "offshore" price for it.

See Table 8.1 for more ways to think about this question.

Proprietary Approaches

Can we develop proprietary processes and approaches that would add value to our positioning?

A focused business strategy provides a platform on which to build unique service offerings that help further distinguish your firm. In fact, the development of proprietary intellectual property is the thing that makes your value proposition "valuable."

This is not an exercise in taking a widely known, widely practiced process and packaging it up with a catchy new name (although it's surprising how many clients react positively to the fact that your firm appears to have a branded, repeatable process). What's really needed to give your positioning credibility is a set of truly unique intellectual capital. It can be a discovery process, a development process, a research approach, a model, or even a signature approach to problem solving.

Smith Brothers, a marketing firm in Pittsburgh specializing in consumer package goods (CPG) offers the national brands they serve a proprietary approach to measuring marketing effectiveness using a series of specially designed metrics and methodologies. This reinforces their reputation as a CPG powerhouse.

High-Value Offerings

How can we maximize the areas in which we can be a brand and minimize the areas in which we are seen as a commodity?

The goal here is to do less of what's easy to find and more of what's hard to find. The near-ubiquitous services in your industry have the least pricing leverage and do the least to distinguish your firm. Much better to invest your energies in what's scarce and in short supply. If you take this concept far enough, you will have achieved the ultimate goal of positioning: creating a category of one.

Intellectual Capital

How can we build a body of intellectual capital that demonstrates our expertise to prospects and clients?

When it comes to intellectual capital, there are really two issues to consider. First, is your firm focused enough to be able to build a strong body of intellectual capital? And second, do you have a systematic way to store and share it? So many firms amass learning around clients, industries, and issues but fail to catalogue it in a way that makes it part of the institutional—not individual—knowledge of the firm. A host of digital asset management online services and software solutions now make this a relatively easy thing to do. All that's needed is the corporate will to do it.

Information Resources

To add to our expertise in our area of focus, do we need access to new or different information resources?

When you transform your firm from being a "full-service" generalist to a positioning strategy as a specialist you'll benefit from joining the appropriate associations, attending the right conferences, and subscribing to syndicated research studies and databases. In fact, it becomes just as important for your firm to participate in its target industries as in its own industry. Unfocused generalist firms don't have this advantage.

Client Selection

Which types of clients best fit our positioning? What kinds of clients do we want more of? What kinds of clients do we want fewer of?

Careful client selection is how you live your positioning. Selecting and cultivating clients that match your positioning is the essence of choosing focus over unfocus.

Does adopting a new positioning mean that you should immediately fire all the clients that don't match it? Of course not. Even for the most successful firm, that would be a little suicidal. Unless you have clients that should be jettisoned for other reasons (unprofitable, difficult to work with, demoralizing to the firm), you can continue to work with your current client base while you build out your new positioning strategy. No client lasts forever—as you lose some of your clients through attrition, replace them with clients who are good positioning fits. (Figure 8.1 suggests a model for how to make good client selection decisions.)

Accountability

How can we enhance our service offering to include tools and approaches to measure success?

There are several reasons why demonstrating accountability is increasingly important for professional knowledge firms. First, clients clearly are demanding it. The demand for more accountability in corporate boardrooms around the world affects everything from marketing results to ROI on legal services. Second, improved measurement of results is foundational to how professional firms will be paid in the future. The coming revolution in compensation—moving from hours worked to value created—will mean firms of all stripes will need to shift the time they currently invest in tracking hours to instead focus on tracking, measuring, and proving results. (For much more about this, see Chapters 9 and 10.)

What Is Core?

One of the greatest challenges to profitability is the perception on the part of clients that some of your firm's services are "commodities." Because clients feel they can get these services down the street—or across the ocean—for less, there is intense pricing pressure on many aspects of professional services.

Unless you do something to add value and turn these perceived commodities into something clients *can't* get down the street, you'll be in a downward spiral of competition for work that doesn't have much of a margin. That's not a very attractive business to be in.

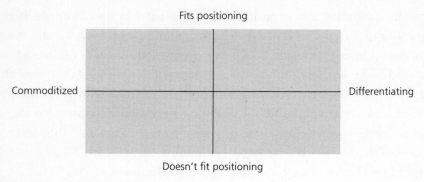

Fits positioning

Commoditized

Differentiating

Doesn't fit positioning

Figure 8.1 Core Competencies

If you step back and look at your services and capabilities, you'll see that there are certain core competencies that are central to the positioning and focus of your firm. For the services that define your value proposition, you should be charging a premium for two reasons:

1. Because they're worth more, and
2. To help offset the smaller margins you make on other services.

One way to define your premium services is to plot your firm's capabilities on the chart in Figure 8.1. Services in the upper right-hand quadrant—those that are differentiating from other firms, plus clearly support your positioning —are not only core to your business model but usually have better pricing leverage.

Another, more radical approach is to decide that you won't offer low-value services at all. This is the philosophy adopted by many (if not most) of the successful new advertising agency start-ups in recent years. They call this approach "big brains, small machine." Their business model is to assemble a group of talented people who provide primarily strategy and ideation, and outsource virtually everything else.

An advertising agency that goes by the very differentiating name Strawberry Frog made headlines several years ago when it launched its firm with a business model that could be called big brains, small machine. When asked how it handles global brands with a relatively small staff, one of the partners explained, "We outsource everything the client views as a commodity."[3] In other words, the firm follows the precept that is increasingly applicable for all professional service firms to either add value and charge accordingly or not do it at all.

The Hollywood Model

Staffing your firm with a core group of very smart people and then assembling teams around them for each project as needed is sometimes referred to as the Hollywood Model. A small but innovative firm in Durham, North Carolina, known as The PARAGRAPH Project is built on this model. Here's how they describe it:

> Our working process is akin to architecture and urban planning. We harvest and apply diverse perspectives to the challenge at hand. Whether an architect or janitor, university professor or high school student, musician or bartender, our solutions are inspired by innovative thinkers in all walks of life.[4]

One of the first questions to ask when attempting the Hollywood Model is, "How do we decide which services to handle in-house and which to outsource?" Spend a morning with your management team and take them through an exercise of listing all the services and capabilities needed by your clients, then evaluating these services against the questions of relevance, differentiation, performance, investment, and repeatability (see Table 8.1).[5]

Table 8.1 Internal versus External Services

Relevance	To what degree is this service necessary to support our positioning strategy?
Differentiation	To what degree does this service help us truly differentiate our firm?
Performance	How would we rate our performance in this area?
Investment	If we're not already excellent in this area, how much of an investment (time, money, resources) would be required to achieve excellence?
Repeatability	Are the outcomes of this activity or capability inherently repeatable and predictable (in terms of time, cost, quality, and so on)?

Based on your analysis of the above, each of these services and capabilities can be assigned to one of three groups:

Core   Done in-house as a core competency of the firm
Partnered   Performed in partnership with another firm
Outsourced   Assigned to an outside resource with little supervision
                from you

If you choose to simply do "everything" for your clients yourself, you will continue to dig yourself deeper into a "high-volume, low-margin" hole. And that violates the first rule of holes, which is, "When you're in one, stop digging."

Aligning Capabilities and Clients

The exercise here will help align your firm's value proposition with its services and client selection.

Clients that match up with all four of the brand boundaries discussed in Chapter 6 are your "A" prospects—the kinds of companies that perfectly fit your value proposition.

Next are the "B" prospects, companies that line up with at least three of your four brand boundaries. Even though they're somewhat less than a perfect fit, these types of clients are generally worth pursuing and cultivating.

"C" prospects match only one of your four brand boundaries, meaning you should say no to this type of company as a client.

Finally, "D" prospects are completely outside all of the brand boundaries, which means you should neither pursue nor accept this type of client.

Remember, client selection is key to a powerful value proposition. To the well-positioned firm, not everyone is a prospect, and the more carefully you select your clients, the stronger your positioning will be in the marketplace.

STAFFING

The area of staffing is about the people side of the business—how the firm selects, organizes, develops, trains, and manages its people. In this area, your positioning strategy should be reflected and executed in each of the ways discussed below.

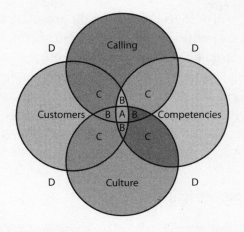

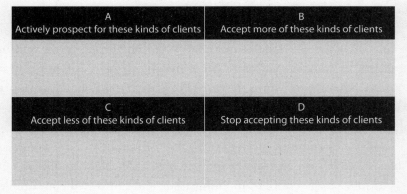

Figure 8.1 Aligning Capabilities and Clients

Roles and Responsibilities

Should roles or responsibilities be redefined to bring the organization into better alignment with our positioning? Do we need different titles to better describe what we do?

New capabilities based on a new positioning often suggests new roles, responsibilities, or even titles for principals, partners, practice leaders, and associates. This is also an opportunity to discard and rename outdated functions—relics from the way firms were organized in the past but not indicative of where they're going in the future.

The central goal, of course, is to bring the organizational structure into alignment with the positioning. The goal is also to explore ways that structure could help further distinguish and differentiate your firm.

In marketing communications firms, for example, the title "media planner" is being replaced by a new title such as "communications planner;" an acknowledgment that the old mass media model of advertising is morphing into a more robust, multichannel approach that includes such things as digital and experiential marketing.

Internal Communication

How can we use all available means to communicate our positioning strategy to everyone in the firm?

Several interesting studies have shown that the quality that is most predictive of a good leader is not education, charisma, or even mentoring abilities; it's communication.[6] Communicating your positioning strategy to every person who works in your firm is essential to living your brand. Marketing professionals call this "internal branding"—helping all associates to understand and support the branding.

Constant communication about the positioning strategy is necessary not only to inform employees and partners about their role in executing it, but to keep the entire team enthusiastic and motivated about building the company brand.

Hiring Standards

Given our value proposition, what criteria should we use when selecting new associates?

A definitive positioning strategy points the way to the skills and talents you need on board to deliver your brand promise. You'll be looking for people with specific experience and credentials, not just a general knowledge of your industry. The recruiting standards and specifications for focused firms go well beyond the standard list of job requirements. For example, a mid-sized multioffice marketing firm by the name of Brunner, which has a strong digital marketing competency, assesses potential employees on the basis of their "digital IQ"—a brief assessment they developed to help identify the most digitally literate associates.

Feedback and Recognition

How can we tie our positioning into an effort to recognize and reward exceptional performance?

Your positioning presents an opportunity to recast employee recognition programs to support your brand. In place of the bland and predictable "employee of the month," you can name an employee recognition award after an important dimension of your positioning strategy. Northlich, a Cincinnati-based advertising firm, has defined one of its brand boundaries—its Calling—as "helping to lift brands to a higher, more relevant place through useful ideas." To help reinforce this idea, the company bestows the "Lift Award" on deserving associates. When you walk through their offices, you'll note the presence of giant paper airplanes to help serve as a reminder.

Professional Development

What can we do to educate our people about our positioning? Do any of our people need to be retrained to better deliver on our value proposition?

Since ongoing professional development is mandatory in many sectors of professional services, this presents a valuable opportunity to impart the knowledge and teach the skills that will help everyone in the firm deliver on the positioning. In addition to the many excellent external resources available, custom in-house training courses can be instrumental in helping all associates live the firm's value proposition.

The multinational marketing service firm Momentum requires all associates to complete a set number of internal training courses designed to help maximize individual effectiveness in the fast-paced world of sales promotion—from project management to software training.

New Associate Orientation

How can we indoctrinate and educate new associates about our positioning?

What better time to inform and motivate new people about the positioning than when they first start at the company? Most firms lack the discipline of a good orientation and assimilation program to begin with, so here's a good reason to recommit to doing a better job in this area.

Performance Planning and Career Development

How can we improve our performance review process and use it to help every associate contribute to our positioning?

As with other people-related initiatives and programs in professional service firms, performance planning and career development often take a backseat to the daily demands of clients. Your positioning strategy presents an opportunity to take a fresh look at your approach to performance reviews, because in addition to the basic behaviors and performance you normally look for in an employee, your value proposition will suggest some other specific areas in which individual people in the firm can contribute to the success of the company. Even a simple question like, "What are you doing to personally help maximize the success of the firm's business strategy?" is an effective way to tie individual performance to company performance.

Internal Communication and Collaboration

Professional service providers think of themselves as being in the "people business," but are among the worst of any industry when it comes to keeping their people informed and involved. Internal communication is the chronic "black hole" in professional service firms. In internal surveys of advertising agencies, for example, internal communication consistently ranks at or near the bottom.[7] It is therefore virtually impossible to overcommunicate to your team and company. Just when you think you're doing too much, you're probably finally starting to do enough.

There's also an opportunity to innovate in this area in order to help your firm stand out. One of the major interactive development and digital marketing firms, Organic, has an online property called "Organism." Whenever new people join Organic, they get a page on Organism and are expected to keep it current with their latest work at the firm. The intent of Organism is to combine elements of a social network, collaboration software, and a company intranet. The result is that associates can locate expertise across the firm's six offices. It also allows project leaders to get informal referrals and recommendations for new team members.[8]

Company intranets and social networks are a powerful way to harness the intellectual capital of your organization. In the consumer marketing world, Best Buy established "Blue Shirt Nation," a social network for their employees to communicate with one another. This gives employees a place where they can all connect and talk about how to solve problems, address customer questions, ask about operational procedures, and just get to know one another. Some firms aggregate and distribute employee tweets as a form of internal communication. Others employ the use of online prediction markets like Intrade to solicit collaboration and feedback, and gauge the success of current and potential initiatives. Existing social networks like Facebook serve as instant (and surprisingly effective) intranets for professional firms of all shapes and sizes.

Aligning People with Positioning

Armed with a well-defined positioning strategy, you have clear direction for the professional development of your associates. To bring your people into alignment with your positioning, make advancement in the firm contingent on completing coursework that supports the development of your value proposition. The most progressive firms have developed online knowledge bases or knowledge exchanges that can help support this effort.

Booz & Company, the global management consulting firm, developed a knowledge exchange where associates post their own educational content. Knowledge bases also can house case histories and lessons learned from after action reviews (see list that follows).

THE AFTER ACTION REVIEW

The after action review (a concept borrowed from the U.S. Army) is a particularly effective way to keep your associates focused on the firm's value proposition.

Here are the key questions in an after action review:

1. Did we equal or exceed the client's expectations?
2. Did we create the expected value with this assignment?
3. How could we have created more value?
4. What were the business results and performance against key metrics?
5. Did we have the right team on this assignment?
6. Did we seek client input and feedback?
7. Did we communicate our accomplishments to the client?
8. In the course of the assignment did we identify future opportunities?
9. Did we stay within time and budget parameters?
10. Could we have captured more value through higher price?
11. If we were doing this type of assignment again, how would we do it?
12. What are the implications for the way we design and deliver our services?
13. How can we communicate the lessons on this assignment to our colleagues?
14. Did this assignment enhance our relationship with this client?
15. What could we do better next time?[9]

Paying for Contributions Instead of Hours

While the professional service community explores the concept of value-based compensation (discussed in Chapter 9), there's another important dimension of value that managers should consider: the value created by their employees.

Just as with current time-based compensation models, the compensation model most professional firms use with their people measures the wrong things.

Using Best Buy again as an example, this electronics retailer experimented with this approach with great success. Based on a program it calls "Results Only Work Environment" employees and managers meet at the beginning of the year to identify specific outcomes that need to be achieved. Employees are given the flexibility to achieve these outcomes by working in the office, at home, or at the beach. There are no timesheets and no requirement to work a certain number of hours. If the desired outcomes are achieved, the company feels it received full value for the money it paid the employee, regardless of the number of hours worked or the number of days in or out of the office. After the first year of this program, Best Buy reported a 35 percent increase in productivity among "Results Only Work Environment" employees, and a 90 percent reduction in turnover.[10]

In another variation of this approach, consider paying bonuses based on the value your associates create for their clients instead of the money they earn for the firm.

Admittedly, this approach takes a lot more effort. But consider how it could help differentiate your firm from countless others in your category.

Management Approach as a Differentiator

Gary Hamel argues that in the "innovation stack" the highest and least addressed form of innovation in most companies is *management* innovation. Most organizations are engaged in some form of product or service innovation or even strategic innovation, but rarely do they consider the way their company is managed to be a source of differentiation for their firm. As examples of management innovation, Hamel points to companies like Whole Foods, W.R. Gore, and Google.[11]

Hamel believes that like Web 2.0, "Management 2.0" is an innovative new management paradigm where:

- Talent counts for more than credentials.
- Everyone has a voice.
- The tools of creativity are widely available.
- Authority is contingent on performance.
- Most everything is decentralized.
- It's easy to experiment.
- Ideas compete equally.
- Resources are free to follow opportunities.
- Decisions are made more by peers than bosses.

Given that many professional service firms are in the business of management consulting, it's more than a little ironic that they rarely employ an inventive management approach themselves. There are, however, a few notable exceptions in the marketing world.

Santa Monica-based advertising firm The Phelps Group is distinguished by an unorthodox approach to people management. Writing in his book *Pyramids Are Tombs*,[12] agency founder Joe Phelps argues that traditional hierarchies in professional firms are counterproductive to collaboration and innovation. In the open office environment of The Phelps Group, everybody—including Joe Phelps—changes offices once a year. Every associate is part of what Phelps calls "self-directed teams" that are directly accountable to their clients; not to agency management.

SELF-PROMOTION

The way your firm promotes itself and prospects for business is dramatically affected by having a clearly defined value proposition. Here are some of the main areas of consideration.

Brand Identity

How does our positioning impact our corporate identity and accompanying materials?

It would be easy to assume that a new positioning would suggest a new corporate identity—possibly a new name, new logo, new color palette, and so on—but that actually is rarely the case. As with the positioning itself, the decision to rename or re-identify a company is strategic, not tactical. Most of the time the current name of the firm is perfectly appropriate and relevant for the new positioning—particularly because so many professional service firms bear the names of their founders. However, the new positioning may be a chance to freshen up what might be a tired-looking logo and bring the brand's graphic standards up-to-date.

Website

How should our value proposition guide the design, content, and architecture of our website?

Your firm's website is indisputably your most important marketing tool. In most cases, 100 percent of your prospective clients will visit your site prior to making a decision about working with your firm. You've made the decision to let your company stand for something instead of trying to stand for everything. Now do the same with your website. Let your positioning be clearly communicated and reflected in both the style and the substance—what you say and how you say it.

Online Marketing and Social Networking

How can we have a more prominent online presence on search engines, blogs, and social networks?

While many professional firms have qualms about "advertising," most clearly understand that they need marketing. Increasingly, the most potent form of marketing exists in the form of your online reputation. Using the power of the Internet and social networks to market your brand is the subject of other books (such as the excellent *Groundswell*), but the point to remember is that your positioning drives what you should be communicating about your firm. As you blog and tweet in an effort to increase interest in your firm, stay on strategy. Your brand is built one post at a time.

Directories

How should we be described and represented in online and offline listings and directories? Are we listed in all the right places?

A new online directory is built practically every day, and it's essential for your brand to be listed and for your positioning to be woven into the description of your firm. Don't fall back into the language of "full service"; describe your brand boundaries, and you'll attract the firms that want you for what you do best.

Business Development Approach

How can we leverage our positioning into more of a "pull" and less of a "push" new business strategy?

When you have a clear, well-marketed focus, the prospects that want and need what you offer usually come to you. The most focused firms get virtually all of their business through reference and referral. Developing an area of expertise and becoming known for it, is "pull" marketing—prospects pull themselves to your value proposition because you offer exactly what they're looking for. The unfocused firms have to resort to the frustrating and ineffective "push" approach—cold calling and playing the so-called numbers game responding to RFPs, RFIs, and RFQs.

Publicity

How can we generate more news and interest in our firm's positioning via publicity, guest columns, and speaking engagements?

Writing, speaking, and publishing are the essence of the "pull" strategy employed by well-positioned firms. It's not only the most effective way to demonstrate you know what you're talking about; it's also usually very useful to your clients and prospects. Even consumer products are beginning to realize that "utility" is the new persuasion.

Industry Recognition

What industry competitions, awards, or other recognition would help us showcase our positioning?

It's easy to assume that the firms that win the most awards and recognition do so simply because they're good. No doubt they're good, but they're also extremely aggressive about getting positive exposure for their brand. An advertising agency known as Fallon McElligott Rice took the advertising world by storm in the 1980s largely thanks to a deliberate, well-funded strategy to enter and win awards competitions. One of the ways the celebrated agency Crispin Porter + Bogusky made its mark on the business world was to get major stories in business magazines and newspapers. Their competitors assumed it was just "lucky Crispin." But behind the scenes, CP+B invested in a staff of internal PR professionals whose only client was the agency.

Unconventional Marketing Approaches

What else can we do to get the attention of our key audiences? How can we use our new positioning as a means of creating positive impressions of our firm?

Rarely does a professional knowledge firm have as good an opportunity to stir up interest in its brand as when it develops a new positioning strategy. It's the perfect opportunity for a feature story in the business section of the newspaper. But there are countless other ways you can generate positive impressions of your firm, limited only by your own creativity. Progressive firms are posting case studies on sites like YouTube and SlideShare. They're conducting instant online polls and sharing the results on LinkedIn. They're uploading examples of their work and projects to Flickr, hosting real-time webinars, and writing entries about the firm on Wikipedia.

How a Clear Positioning Strategy Helps You Move from "Push" to "Pull"

Ask the leader of any professional services firm what he or she dislikes the most in the area of business development and the answer will almost always be the same: cold calling prospects. Not only is this the most dreaded activity among C-level professional services executives, it's also among the least effective.

Cold calling has always produced only modest results, and today's avoidance-enabling technology only makes it easier for prospects to hide from your phone calls and ignore your emails. The dynamics that make it more difficult to reach a client's prospective customers are the same forces that make it harder for professional firms to reach their own prospective customers: media proliferation, multitasking, message overload, and short attention spans.

If you feel guilty for not spending enough time cold calling and cold emailing, here's a really good excuse to stop: It doesn't work.

Peter Drucker preached that a good marketing program makes sales irrelevant. "The aim of marketing," says Drucker, "is to make selling superfluous."[13] In other words, the goal of marketing is to make a product so relevant and compelling that it literally sells itself. If you think this is mere hyperbole, consider the outrageously successful iPhone. Can you imagine ever seeing an iPhone salesman? Instead, eager customers are lined up in front of Apple and AT&T stores for hours.

If professional firms spent more time and energy on making and *marketing* a relevant, differentiated "product," they could spend a lot less time and energy trying to *sell* it. The most differentiated firms spend the least amount of time prospecting. Instead of chasing new business, wouldn't you prefer to have it chase you?

The only limit is the amount of creativity you apply to marketing your own brand. So stop thinking sales and start thinking marketing, which starts with how the product (your agency) is positioned in the marketplace. Trade the time and money you spend "selling" your brand and invest it instead in *differentiating and marketing* your brand, and you'll get a much better return on your investment.

Creating an Unlevel Playing Field

Most business development professionals have heard the phrase, "New business is a numbers game." As the theory goes, you need a lot of times at bat (meaning you need to take a lot of swings) in order to hit the occasional home run. This school of business development believes that professional firms need to pursue and pitch a certain number of new business opportunities in order to win their fair share.

It's a logical argument. But it's wrong.

It's precisely because most firms view new business as a numbers game that many industries have created and perpetuated the ridiculously cumbersome and ineffective "review" process. Firms scramble to respond to as many RFPs as they possibly can, knowing that they will make the cut on only so many, and eventually will win only a small percentage of the reviews in which they are invited to participate.

The goal of most competitive reviews is to "level the playing field." These cattle call–style reviews attempt to line up and compare firms on a set of common characteristics. Your job is to unlevel the playing field. Rather than showing how well you compare, you should go out of your way to show how you don't compare.

You're not playing the lottery here. Instead of being at the mercy of the law of averages, you can dramatically improve your chances of winning with a relevant and differentiated positioning.

Instead of investing the necessary mental energy to actually position themselves uniquely in the marketplace, most firms try to improve the law of averages through cosmetics. They opt for a more finely produced RFP response, nicer looking offices, or a more decked-out presentation room.

But deep down inside, most executives realize that this isn't really the answer. Having a clear idea of what you're selling is the answer.

A Multidimensional Marketing Approach

Most of the firms that constantly kick themselves for not devoting enough effort to "prospecting" are the same ones that have devoted below-average resources to marketing their own brand. That's no coincidence.

In place of a traditional new business prospecting program, you need to make sure one or more people in your firm are assigned to implement a real-time multidimensional marketing program that includes:

- Building and maintaining a permission-based list of prospects and influencers and sending appropriate periodic emailings and mailings.

- Ensuring that the website is constantly refreshed and updated with information, examples, case studies, biographies, and more.
- Constantly updating and maintaining both offline and online directory listings, including industry-specific directories, business directories, and paid listing services.
- Regularly reading and posting to appropriate blogs and publications. Fostering relationships with relevant bloggers and online publishers.
- Identifying, buying, and managing URLs for landing pages that can be used by your firm.
- Developing and maintaining company profile pages on LinkedIn, Facebook, and other appropriate social networks.
- Seeing that information about the firm is published in Wikipedia, which is increasingly influential as an information resource on companies and brands.
- Overseeing an online search marketing program for the firm, including identifying and purchasing keywords and phrases.
- Identifying and coordinating online advertising opportunities on appropriate websites, blogs, and so on.
- Maximizing the firm's online presence by proactively posting materials, videos, photos, and podcasts on sites such as YouTube, iTunes, Flickr, SlideShare, Scribd, Screencast.
- Actively identifying opportunities to publicize the firm's intellectual capital by monitoring reporter queries using services like HARO.
- Creating a positive presence for the firm on websites and blogs that are influential in attracting and recruiting top talent.
- Appointing "brand ambassadors" in the firm whose job is to blog and tweet on behalf of the firm, making sure that all content is focused on supporting the firm's positioning strategy.
- Measuring and refining the firm's online presence using analytics tools such as Google Analytics, Alexa, Technorati, and so on, and monitoring the success of the firm's social media program through the use of third-party applications such as Radian6 or BuzzMetrics.

Today, one of the most critical aspects of a professional firm's business development function is to earn a prominent place for your firm's brand in the online conversation about your industry. It's one thing to have an effective website; it's quite another to have an effective web *presence*. Research shows that less than 50 percent of your organic ranking on search engines comes from what you do on your website. Most of your ranking is determined by the other things you do (or don't do) online.

SYSTEMS

It's sometimes not immediately obvious that even the firm's process and procedures can present opportunities for differentiation. Here are some of the main questions to consider.

Resource Allocation

Does our positioning suggest new or different ways in which resources (both human and financial) should be allocated in our firm?

A positioning strategy has major implications for the way resources are deployed in the firm. It might suggest the combination or dissolution of certain functions or practice areas. Cleveland-based Liggett-Stashower realized that given its focus as building products marketing experts it would make sense to take down the wall that separated the advertising practitioners from the PR practitioners. Its people were redeployed in new roles as counselors who could help advise clients in both paid and nonpaid marketing strategies.

Pricing Practices

Based on our positioning, have we clearly defined what we're really selling and what our clients are really buying?

The question here is: What can you do to change your pricing practices to better reflect your desired position in the marketplace? Specialists can command better prices than generalists.

Processes

Which processes define and differentiate our firm, and how can we further develop them?

Besides being a facilitator, process also can be a differentiator. A few marketing communications firms have experimented with Six Sigma and ISO9000 programs—mostly at the request of their clients—with unexpectedly positive results.

Project Management

In what ways can we redevelop our approach to project management that will help us deliver on our positioning?

Professional project management practices have long been the standard in IT consulting firms and digital marketing agencies. The complexities of information technology and digital marketing require it. But even the softer side of professional services can benefit from better project management practices, and actually can help the firm more effectively deliver its value proposition.

Scope Management

Can we apply more attention and innovation to managing the scope of our assignments and ensure that the scope is aligned with our core strengths?

Besides poor pricing, scope creep is another major profit drain in professional knowledge firms. The sad fact is that most firms lack either the ability, the will, or the courage to track changes in scope and then ask to get paid for it. Scope management relates to positioning in the sense that the scope definition should reflect what the firm knows it can deliver. Too many firms overpromise and then underdeliver, which only serves to erode your most valuable asset: your reputation.

Quality Control

How do we ensure that our work meets the standards we have set for ourselves in a way that supports and adds credibility to our value proposition?

Quality assurance (QA) isn't just for automobile manufacturing. It is now one of the essential responsibilities of professional project managers. As technology plays a greater role in the deliverables of professional service companies, quality control will be key factor in maintaining the reputation of the firm.

Intellectual Property

How can we use our positioning as an opportunity to develop and own more of our own intellectual property?

Too many professional service firms are in the business of providing "work for hire." But by embracing a clear positioning and developing deep expertise in a particular area, professional firms have an opportunity to create, own, and license more of the intellectual property they create.

Knowledge Bases

How can we better catalogue what we have learned about our area of expertise and make it available to all associates?

As your firm continues to develop a body of knowledge and experience in its chosen area of focus, it's essential to make the information available 24/7 to the associates who need it.

Policies

Are any of our policies in conflict with our positioning?

Finally, your firm must scour its policies, operating procedures, and employee handbooks to ensure that the operating and human resources practices of the firm are in line with the desired positioning. Ironically, some of the marketing firms that promise inventive digital marketing solutions to their clients actually restrict employee access to social networking sites for fear that their people will be playing on their computers instead of "working."

Process Is Just as Important for Knowledge Workers

It's a popular misconception that professional firms don't need to devote as much effort to the question of process as the companies that manufacture a product. Not true. Just like any other kind of work, knowledge work can benefit from better systems and procedures. Consultant Jack Bergstrand, who has studied this question extensively, makes this compelling argument:

> Because of the invisible and ever-changing nature of the work, knowledge workers are sometimes not held to the same results-oriented standards as manual workers. But, they need to be. Knowledge work that doesn't systematically result in tangible output wastes scare resources. Studies and projects that don't get implemented are a waste of time and money. Good ideas that are not implemented also waste resources. With the rapid half-life of knowledge, good ideas won't be good for long, even in the best circumstances. For this reason, speed matters with knowledge work much more than with manual work.

Bergstrand further frames his argument this way:

> Does it take your large company a couple of weeks to set up a meeting with key people because their calendars are so busy or because they won't be in the office for awhile? And even then, is it difficult to get contentious tradeoffs made and decisions acted upon? If so, you are either in trouble or headed toward it. It has never been clearer. Unless your company is a monopoly, if your enterprise can't improve its knowledge work productivity and reinvent itself faster, your firm's best years are behind it.[14]

The Institute of Practitioners of Advertising (IPA) in the UK recently published a position paper called "Magic and Logic," which argues that clients are willing to give agencies credit for being effective in the "magic" side of their business—providing ideas to grow brands—but not in the "logic" side—effective project management. The paper points out that "in most agencies, 90 percent of the management focus is on the *magic*, but 90 percent of the client's money is spent on the *logic*," and that most of the problems between clients and agencies appear to be in the logic department. [15]

The father of the quality movement, W.E. Deming, believed that 85 percent of workers' effectiveness is determined by the systems they work within.[16] If he's right—and he well may be—professional firms have to pay a lot more attention to this essential question.

We tend to think of systems as things that run in the background, but the opportunity is to turn some of what we consider "background processes" into "identity processes"—processes that actually help define and differentiate the firm. Most of us also tend to view process as a necessary evil: a cost and a liability. But a unique, differentiating process actually can be an asset. Rather than just costing money, process innovations can make money.[17]

One such example is the advertising firm Deutsch in New York, which has responded to the needs of its high-profile retail clients by adding a "night shift" that allows the firm to provide 24/7 service. Even in the fast-paced ad world, this is a form of operational innovation that distinguishes this firm from direct competitors.

Intellectual Property Ownership

Advertising agencies in particular are in the habit of performing "work for hire," wherein the client owns the rights to all the intellectual property created by the agency. But as relationships get shorter and margins thinner, agencies are experimenting with different approaches to intellectual property (IP) ownership. Besides being good business, it's an example of a differentiating business practice.

One notable example is the firm Anomaly, which as a matter of principle seeks to own or share in the ownership of the work it does for its clients. Says the magazine *Creative Review*, "Anomaly is defiantly not an 'ad agency.' The company sets store by developing its own intellectual property, which it can license to clients in return for share in revenues. Their aspiration is to be a product-developing IP company, marketing their own portfolio of IP as well as doing that for major brands."[18]

STAGING

Your firm's place of business—both physical and virtual—is an important manifestation of your positioning strategy. Every touch point associated with your brand must sync with your value proposition. Set aside ten minutes to see what your clients and prospects experience when they call your firm (especially after hours). Listen to recorded greetings from your key associates. Try to navigate through the automated phone extension directory. Then look at emails signed by various people within the firm. Some may have a company logo, some not; some are plain vanilla formatting, some look very professional. Next, assemble a collection of online memos, reports, recommendations, and proposals. It most likely will be a mishmash of different formats and fonts—most missing the company logo altogether.

Your brand has many touch points, and each one creates an impression—positive or negative. Your positioning affords you opportunities to infuse all of these touch points with the right look, feel, and tone. Start by asking the following questions.

First Impressions

Are we sending the right message about our brand when others make contact with us? Are we using all available channels—both physical and virtual—to communicate our positioning to clients and prospects?

Offices

Does our place of business communicate and reinforce our positioning? Do we have a standard for how offices are designed, furnished, and decorated?

Working Environment

How can we do a better job of creating a working environment that is more compatible withour brand? Does our desired brand suggest a type of office layout or structure?

Tools and Resources

Have we armed our associates with the things they need to do their best work and live our positioning? What tools or resources would help us be even more expert and effective in our chosen area of focus?

Technology

Have we leveraged available hardware and software to create a competitive point of difference for the firm? Do we maximize the use of online services to share, collaborate, and communicate?

Digital Asset Management

Do we have an effective means of organizing and cataloguing the files and digital assets that our associates and clients need? Is our intellectual capital readily accessible and is it organized in such as way as to support our positioning?

Virtual Office

Have we moved beyond defining work as "being at your desk"? Are our associates enabled to work effectively anywhere in the world?

Brand Touch Points

Have we considered all of the other physical and virtual touch points of our brand? Have we done a thorough audit of all the ways our clients and prospects come in contact with our brand?

The Virtual Associate

Architect Clive Wilkinson, who designed the famed Googleplex, says business has morphed from an industrial economy to a service economy to what is now an *idea* economy. Offices and workers are no longer bound by paper. So Wilkinson believes the knowledge worker needs:

1. A place to sit comfortably
2. A place to put stuff
3. A place to connect with people (physically or virtually)[19]

Enter the age of the virtual knowledge worker. Close to half of IBM's workforce has no formal office. Increasingly, the virtual worker is an important part of progressive firms in all industries. This has a significant impact on the way firms equip their associates. Mobile knowledge workers don't need office furniture and won't consume any office coffee, but they do require state-of-the-art technology to do their jobs well. Instead of needing a corporate infrastructure (offices and conference rooms, for example), they need to be able to build their own *personal* infrastructure (laptop, mobile phone, online conferencing services, and so on.).[20]

The advertising business is noted for its willingness to experiment with different work environments. In the UK, a firm with the memorable name Mother has no private offices (and no doors, for that matter). Instead, all agency partners and associates work from a huge concrete table. Everyone in the firm is mobile and agile, able to work from any spot in the agency. Besides doing an excellent job of equipping their people with a strong personal infrastructure, Mother pays everyone a daily "self-improvement bonus" that can be used for anything from books to gym memberships. The agency offers two types of weekly massages, free hot lunches, a winter ski trip, three-month sabbaticals, plus days off for birthdays and the day after Mother's Day (naturally). The firm says fewer than 10 percent of its 165 employees leave annually, compared with the 30 percent average in U.S. agencies.[21]

The Martin Agency, based in Richmond, Virginia, is considered to be one of the creative leaders in the United States. The process of building a reputation for creativity and innovation is a taller task in a place like Richmond than in New York or Chicago, which is why in the early days of the agency it erected a sign at its entrance that read: "Nobody comes to Richmond for the restaurants."

The Senses and Your Firm's Brand

The way your brand is physically represented actually involves four areas. Capitalize on opportunities to differentiate yourself in as many of these ways as possible.

See: Iconography, shapes, colors, images, office décor

While most firms prominently display their logo in their reception areas, only a few take advantage of the immense power of visual imagery to create an instant impression of the company. A marketing firm in Colorado specializing in agriculture marketing has made its desks and office dividers from old farm equipment. An agency in southern California has even taken its branding program to the parking lot, where signs at each client parking space display a message like, "Please park precisely between the lines. Brand alignment is everything around here." A firm in Kansas City has even created its own postage stamp (a feature now offered by the U.S. Postal Service).

Feel: Shapes, texture, depth, space

Texture in particular is often an overlooked aspect of the physical manifestation of the brand. The use of certain wall coverings, floor coverings, countertops, and even paper stock can create a tactile experience associated with your brand. A Midwest firm specializing in digital marketing uses corrugated cardboard as not only a rough-hewn office design standard but a way to bind and package its proposals and credentials.

Hear: Music, rhythm, sound, recorded messages

What does it say about your firm when your clients enter a long space of silence when placed on hold? Marketing firms are particularly good in this area, using the "on hold" experience as an opportunity to entertain. When your call is transferred by one Atlanta-based agency, you'll hear a series of tongue-in-cheek messages about how the firm can help you benefit from the "capitalist revolution."

Smell: Aromas, olfactory sensations

Scent is becoming "the elixir of branding" because it has the power to trigger memory and potentially create a more pleasant customer experience. When you stay at a Westin hotel, you'll experience the official Westin aroma: "Westin White Tea, a blend of green tea, geranium, green ivy, black cedar, and freesia."

EXECUTING A POSITIONING STRATEGY WITH ALIGNMENT TEAMS

Even with the leadership of the firm personally involved, it will take all hands on deck to execute your positioning strategy. One effective method is to form a small "alignment team" for each of the above areas. Select a group of doers, not a group of talkers—people who are known for getting things done. (These people may or may not be your most senior managers.)

Appoint a talented senior executive to lead each of these teams, and recruit appropriate associates throughout the firm to serve on these teams and take ownership of the strategic initiatives necessary to bring the positioning to life.

These teams should have representatives from different functions within the organization, including a sponsor, leader, manager, and members.

Sponsor: A principal of the firm whose role it is to advise the team and authorize the expenditure of the firm's time and resources.

Leader: A senior executive whose job it is to provide direction to the alignment team, lead and moderate discussions, make decisions, and prioritize initiatives.

Manager: An associate who is talented in the area of organization and planning whose job it is to manage the logistics of the alignment team, including organizing meetings, assigning due dates, and tracking the progress of assignments.

Members: Various associates (no more than three) from different functions and departments who will be given responsibility for executing the initiatives of the alignment team.

In addition to this organization, make sure that each major initiative has an "owner"—an individual on the alignment team who will take personal ownership of the initiative.

The alignment team's job will be to:

- Help identify the needed initiatives in its area of responsibility.
- Realistically prioritize the initiatives.
- Design an action plan to carry out the initiatives.
- Recruit help from other associates to execute the initiatives.
- Regularly monitor the success of the initiatives and report to management.

The Team Agreement

Because of the tendency for professionals to "back burner" the work of the firm (versus client work), it's critical that every alignment team member commit to the following:

1. We agree to devote at least three hours per week to our alignment team responsibilities.
2. We agree to meet regularly to review assignments and due dates.
3. We agree to arrive at meetings on time and to devote our full attention to the subject at hand (versus our mobile devices).
4. We agree to respect one another's time by showing up to meetings prepared.
5. We agree to leave every meeting with a clear set of actions, due dates, and responsibilities.
6. We agree to put first things first and avoid wasting our time debating the small points of small issues.

7. We agree that in between meetings, we will continue to collaborate using one of the many available online collaboration tools (such as Basecamp).

8. We agree to routinely keep the firm's management informed of our progress.

Prioritizing the Initiatives

If everything is important, nothing is important. It's vital that each of the alignment teams prioritize its initiatives to stay focused on the "vital few versus the trivial many." Here's a good filter for this purpose:

Impact = Effect on the long-term success of the organization

Investment = Required expenditure of time, money, or resources

Table 8.1   Prioritizing Initiatives

A High Impact Low Investment	B High Impact High Investment
C Low Impact Low Investment	D Low Impact High Investment

Weatherproof Your Strategy

Most teams and most initiatives fail for a very familiar set of reasons. As you get underway with your alignment teams, make an effort to "weatherproof" your initiatives by asking the following questions up front:

1. Do the teams have the required knowledge and skills to accomplish their initiatives?

2. Do they have the right attitude and motivation?
3. Do they have not just the responsibility but also the accompanying rights?
4. Do they have adequate resources, including a budget?
5. Do the teams have agreed-upon deadlines and specific individuals responsible for specific assignments?
6. Is there a reporting mechanism that will help keep the teams accountable for their progress?
7. Most important, is it clear to the teams that the management of the firm is personally involved in and committed to these initiatives?

When given a challenging assignment, the most common question asked by those responsible is almost always, "How?"

The answer to how is "yes." So says Peter Block in his excellent exploration of effectiveness. The questions you really should be asking are:

Not . . .	**. . . But**
How do you do it?	Do I want to do it?
How long will it take?	How much do I want to do it?
How do you get people to go along with it?	How much do I want to change?
How have others done this?	Am I up to the personal challenge?

The question, ultimately, is not about practicality but *personal commitment*. The problems and challenges are not "out there"—they're "in here." We must become the subject instead of the object.[22]

REBUILDING YOUR SHIP WHILE AT SEA

Unless you're launching a completely new company, you don't really have the luxury of shutting down your business while you reconstruct your value proposition. You have to rebuild your ship while you're running at cruising speed, which requires that you both support and deconstruct your business model simultaneously.

Implementing a new value proposition is a process, not an event. In fact, it's a process that's never really done. There are always new and better ways to bring your practices into alignment with your positioning.

In professional knowledge firms, clients always come first. So make sure the key members on your team understand that they have an important client that will take the best they have to give: your own brand.

CHAPTER 9

Getting Paid for Creating Value

N ow more than ever, professional knowledge firms are struggling to preserve their margins. Many executives believe that a big part of the problem is their firms' chronic tendency to exceed estimated hours on client relationships and assignments. As a result, professional firms are feverishly trying to improve their estimating systems while at the same time pressing their accounting departments for increasingly detailed analyses of how employee time is spent. They are on a quest to improve how their firms estimate, track, and bill their time.

The problem, of course, isn't the practices; it's the paradigm.

The correct paradigm for a professional knowledge firm is that you're selling business results, not time. Clients don't buy your efforts; they buy the outcomes the efforts produce. Your internal costs have nothing to do with the external value you create for your clients.

A cost-based paradigm treats knowledge workers as though they're hourly wage laborers from the industrial age. The value-based paradigm considers knowledge workers to be capable of creating incredible wealth and value for their clients—irrespective of hours worked.

The clock is an outdated metaphor in an age of knowledge work. It's really a relic of the industrial age when it really mattered whether you were "on the clock" because it meant you were present on the assembly line "creating value." But knowledge workers can create value at their desk, sitting in a Starbucks, or taking a shower, because the value they create is in the form of intellectual capital. Knowledge work requires a different set of assumptions about productivity.

THE PERILS OF COST-BASED COMPENSATION

Time-based compensation is wrong because it places importance on efforts instead of results. It essentially says, "We spent this many hours, pay us this much money." But when you're buying a new car, do you really care how many hours it took to build it?

When a client relationship is based on hours and costs, it fosters a production mentality instead of an entrepreneurial spirit. That's because it keeps the firm in a mindset of dutifully working on a set of predefined tasks. Value-based compensation gives the firm a completely different outlook on how it spends its time because it provides an incentive to think—not just do.

A compensation structure based on hours actually worked provides a *disincentive* for the firm to invest extra thought and energy. Ironically, the only way the firm can earn more is to increase costs to the client by increasing its hours. Conversely, as the firm becomes more efficient on a client's business, its income goes down. Doesn't make much sense, does it?

What's an Hour Worth?

A time-based approach also assumes that all hours are equally valuable, when we know that sometimes an hour of time can produce remarkable value, and sometimes it can produce absolutely nothing. But the client pays for that hour just the same. The truth is, not all hours are created equal, and billable hours don't build successful companies.

The fact that an assignment is expected to take 53 hours of firm time bears no relationship to the value to the client. The 53 hours might result in ineffective work. Did the cost of the time translate into value for the client? Not necessarily.

Similarly, imagine that your firm invests 30 minutes in developing a brilliant idea that has the potential to transform your client's business. Again, was the cost of the time equal to the value for the client?

You must help everyone in your firm—from the accounting department to client service—understand this concept: There is absolutely no relationship between cost and value. Otherwise a rock from a diamond mine and a diamond from a diamond mine would have the same value, because the cost of extracting them was exactly the same. An 8 × 10-foot oil painting by Joe Schwartz and an 8 × 10-foot painting by Vincent Van Gogh would have exactly the same value because the cost of materials and the time required to paint them were exactly the same.

Leaders of professional knowledge firms must come to grips with what it is they are really selling. You don't sell time any more than fine artists sell oil paint and canvases.

In new business situations, one ad firm says, "We're not in the business of selling time—we sell momentum for your business." If pressed on their timesheet-less approach, their response is, "Do you want to haggle over hours, time, and costs, or do you want the ideas that will give momentum to your brand?"[1]

Professionals should be paid based on their talent, not their costs. Think about your favorite actor. Cate Blanchett doesn't get paid for a movie based on her timesheets, but rather her box office draw.

Advertising practitioner Rory Sutherland gives an example of problem solving not related to time:

> Last week I was in a meeting with a pharmaceutical company. We learned that the biggest problem faced by medicine overall was not a scientific one but a human one—non-compliance. People not completing their course of antibiotics. Easy, we said. Just make 20 of the pills white and four of them blue. Tell people to take the white ones first, followed by the blue ones.[2]

What's the value of that idea? Certainly not the 15 minutes it took an experienced practitioner to come up with it. A more conventional approach would have been to recommend a multiyear, multimillion dollar advertising campaign to "educate" consumers about why it's important to take all their medicine. Instead, both the client and the firm benefit from a much better idea.

Estimating Costs Is Not Pricing

Over the years, your firm undoubtedly has become expert in costing. Based on hours, you know exactly what your salary and overhead are on a project. In other words, you know the cost. But do you know the value? It's a different question—and a much more important one.

When you walk around your firm asking each team member to estimate their hours on an upcoming project, you're working only on the cost side of the equation. In fact, that's all an estimate really is—a tally of anticipated costs. It has nothing to do with the value to the client. Estimating is not pricing.

CHANGING THE LANGUAGE

There's no doubt that changing to a value-based compensation (VBC) approach requires a change in financial management, but mostly it involves a change in thinking. You'll never succeed in implementing the *practice* until you first accept the *theory*—and that requires using different language when talking about compensation and client relationships.

Not efficiency	But effectiveness
Not the cost of inputs	But the value of outputs
Not internal measurements	But external measurements

Instead of negotiating price, you should be negotiating value. Clients are not price conscious, they are value conscious.

A digital firm tells the story of an online retailer who was struggling to increase its online sales. This client's website featured a simple online order form with two fields, two buttons, and one link. Yet, it turns out this form was preventing customers from purchasing products. After conducting a few simple usability tests, the executives of the digital firm learned that most customers didn't want to be required to "register" on the site in order to make a purchase; they just wanted to give their credit card information and buy the product. So they took away the "Register" button and put in its place a button that simply says "Continue." This small change resulted in the number of purchasers increasing by 45 percent. In the first year, the site saw an additional $300,000,000 in sales.[3] This example of professional services, now known in the industry as the "$300 Million Button," sharply illustrates how time is not related to value. The firm spent its intellectual capital, not its time, in solving the problem and in the process created tremendous value for its client. Time and value are not in any way related.

This phenomenon is related to the apocryphal story of the washing machine repairman who responds to a service call armed not only with a tool bag, but with 20 years of washing machine repair experience. After spending less than five minutes looking at the machine, he takes a hammer from his tool bag and issues a precise blow to the front panel of the washer, which instantly fixes the problem. He then takes out his invoice form and hands a bill for $100 to the homeowner. Of course the reaction of the homeowner was incredulous. "How could you charge me $100? You've only been working for five minutes, and all you did was hit my washer with a hammer." "Well," says the repairman, "it's $1 for the swing of the hammer and $99 for knowing where to hit." In categories from appliance repair to tax preparation, the issue is never efficiency, but rather effectiveness. Not "How long did this take?" but rather "Did you achieve the desired result?"

PRICING AS A CORE COMPETENCY

So now that you've mastered the art of costing, it's time to become just as good at pricing. In fact, pricing should be elevated to the same level of importance as other core functions of the firm. In manufacturing firms, pricing is a decision, not a process, and it's done by professionals, not salespeople, accountants, or even the CEO.

The first step in pricing based on value instead of costs is to understand the nature of value, including how, when, and where value is created.

The problem is that almost all professional knowledge firms are looking in the wrong place for value. Their compensation agreements are based on hours worked, FTEs assigned, and costs incurred. Hours and costs look *inside* the firm, but value is created *outside* the firm. In other words, value is created outside your four walls. Professional firms and their clients, therefore, usually are looking in the wrong place for the basis of pricing and compensation.

If you don't understand how you create value for your clients, you'll never succeed in being paid for it.

A survey conducted by the American Association of Advertising Agencies asked agencies, "What information do you track?" Here's what they said:

Job estimates	98%
Labor hours and costs	94%
Staffing plans	82%
Client business results	22%[4]

These results make it painfully clear that agencies believe value is created inside, rather than outside, their organizations, because they're paying close attention to internal activities and very little attention to external outcomes.

WHY A VALUE-BASED APPROACH IS IN THE CLIENT'S BEST INTEREST

If you were a client paying your law firm for outcomes instead of hours, would you expect that the firm would be better or worse at the following:

1. Gaining an understanding of your business
2. Clarifying expectations
3. Planning

4. Managing
5. Communicating with you
6. Providing you with proactive thinking

The answer in every case is, of course, better. So why exactly would intelligent clients be opposed to this approach? They wouldn't.

Value-based compensation works primarily for one major reason: It aligns the interests of the firm and the client. Both parties are working to achieve the same things. You both have similar financial incentives.

The Chronic Disadvantages of Hourly Billing

The VeraSage Institute, whose mission to bury the billable hour, has compled an impressive list of disadvantages of hourly billing:

- Hourly billing misaligns the interest of the firm and the client—the client wants its work done effectively, whereas the firm wants to log more hours.
- It focuses on efforts, inputs, hours, costs, and activities, rather than outputs, results, and value.
- It places the transaction risk on the client.
- It fosters a production mentality, not an entrepreneurial spirit.
- It encourages the hoarding of hours and decreases delegation, leading to surgeons piercing ears.
- It penalizes technological advances, lessening a firm's revenue if it performs work more effectively.
- It commoditizes the firm's intellectual capital into one inadequate hourly rate, denying a firm the opportunity to differentiate itself from the competition.
- It doesn't take into account the risk the firm is assuming in working for clients. Risk is not priced by the hour. (Actuaries have an axiom: There is no such thing as bad risks, only bad premiums.)
- It places an artificial ceiling on a firm's net income, since there are only so many hours in a day—indeed, in a lifetime.
- It creates bureaucracy. Maintaining time and billing programs consumes a sizable portion of the firm's gross revenue. These resources are better spent pricing on purpose.

■ It diminishes quality of life for associates of the firm. No one became a professional to bill the most hours, but rather to achieve something important. (Knowledge workers resent having to account for every six minutes of their day, as if their leaders do not trust them to do the work and the right thing.)

Source: The VeraSage Institute, 2009

THE ALIGNMENT OF INCENTIVES

As discussed briefly, some professional services are now "purchased" by procurement professionals within client organizations. While this is a worrisome trend that hints at the perceived "commoditization" of professional services, there are some strategies to fight back. If clients employ professional buyers (procurement agents), shouldn't service firms employ professional sellers? And shouldn't it be the job of professional sellers to know not only how to deal with pricing objections, but how to structure a deal that will solve *both* parties' issues?

It's easy to assume that procurement professionals are interested only in saving money by getting your services as cheaply as possible. But procurement exists as a function to secure *value* for the company. Consequently, procurement departments drag professional service firms through a series of detailed, invasive questions about their process, cost structures, competencies, experience, financial strength, and more, all with one central goal in mind: *to make sure the firm is capable of delivering what it says it can deliver.*

In the faulty world of time-based compensation, the client organization really has no other way to evaluate or ensure performance. As long as professional firms continue to price their services based on costs (hours) instead of value, procurement professionals will always be looking for compliance to their process as a means of evaluating whether a firm is really, truly capable of delivering what it promises.

In the end, procurement has a laboriously detailed process for selecting service providers because of the total lack of alignment of economic incentives.

In fact, in the current cost-based system, there is a real *misalignment* of incentives. Firms actually have an incentive to spend more time, not less.

Next time you're working with a procurement department, ask, "What if we proposed a form of compensation in which the economic incentives of both parties were in near-perfect alignment?" An associate of mine recently asked such a question of a respected procurement professional of a major company. His response? "Then there would be no need for compliance to our detailed process." My colleague then asked, "So why not just bypass the process and go directly to what it's supposed to accomplish; alignment of incentives?" He was compelled to agree that this is actually the ultimate job of procurement.

If you want to disarm procurement, you must first walk away from the notion that you're selling time. Then give procurement the assurance it needs right up front by proposing compensation based on your ability to create the value it seeks in the first place.

Taking Responsibility for Value

Professional firms typically have senior executives in charge of all major functions except pricing. Because pricing is not accounting, the chief financial officer in the firm is often the worst—not the best—choice to head up the pricing function. Professional knowledge firms should appoint a confident executive to the post of chief value officer whose job would be: Understanding the firm's basic value proposition and how it creates value for its clients.

- Ensuring that the firm prices on purpose, according to the value received by the client, not the costs incurred by the firm.

- Keeping the firm focused on profitable client relationships, not merely taking on new clients to fuel nonprofitable revenue growth.

- Establishing all company pricing and compensation policies, including professional guarantees.

- Improving scope definition and management and ensuring that all scope of work discussions are preceded by a discussion of scope of value.

- Overseeing all pricing and compensation agreements for major client assignments and relationships.

- Presenting pricing proposals and negotiating with client buyers, including procurement professionals when necessary.

- Constructing and experimenting with various forms of value-based compensation agreements with clients.

- Identifying the right kind of client (current or prospective) for compensation agreements based on specific outcomes.

- Working with other associates to develop, test, and track key predictive indicators that form the basis of outcome-based agreements.

- Developing approaches that will enable the firm to own more of its own intellectual property and to derive ongoing revenues from its use.

- Making pricing for value a core competency by ensuring that the firm is engaged in continuous learning around pricing and value, and teaching every associate the importance of pricing for value.

- Establishing a pricing knowledge base and sharing pricing and compensation success stories throughout the firm.

- Playing the role of "bad cop" when it comes to pricing by dealing with price objections from clients and client organizations. (Because the number of pricing objections is finite, the CVO should have answers for all of them.)

- Helping to keep the firm focused on effectiveness instead of just efficiency, including establishing effectiveness tools, reports, and metrics in place of traditional time-based efficiency tools and metrics.

- Grading current clients and determining which clients should be "outplaced" due to lack of profitability. (This permits the firm to then focus on providing more value-added services to better clients that are less price-sensitive and more valuable to the firm.)

- Conducting after action reviews at the end of major client assignments and relationships in order to assess what was learned and how the firm could have priced the work better.

- Becoming members of professional pricing organizations, reading, attending seminars, and networking with other pricing professionals in order to develop intellectual capital and adopt best practices.

Thanks to my colleague Ron Baker, co-founder of the VeraSage Institute and author of many excellent books on how professional firms can create and capture value, for most of the points in this list.

CREATING A VIRTUOUS CIRCLE

In economics, a virtuous circle or a vicious circle is a complex of events that reinforces itself through a feedback loop. A *virtuous* circle has favorable results, and a *vicious* circle has detrimental results. Both systems of events have feedback loops in which each iteration of the cycle reinforces the previous one. These cycles will continue in the direction of their momentum until an external factor intervenes and breaks the cycle. (See Figures 9.1 and 9.2).

The goal of professional service firms should be to break the vicious circle of hourly billing—a system that misaligns the interests of the firm and its clients. By changing your paradigm about pricing and value, your firm can be one of the catalysts that initiates a virtuous circle in your industry.

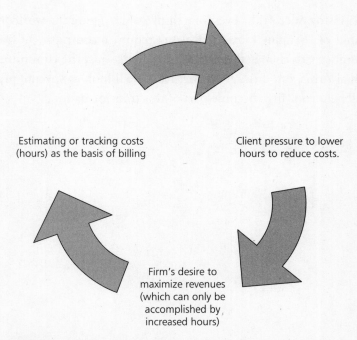

Estimating or tracking costs
(hours) as the basis of billing

Client pressure to lower
hours to reduce costs.

Firm's desire to
maximize revenues
(which can only be
accomplished by
increased hours)

Figure 9.1 The Current Vicious Compensation Circle

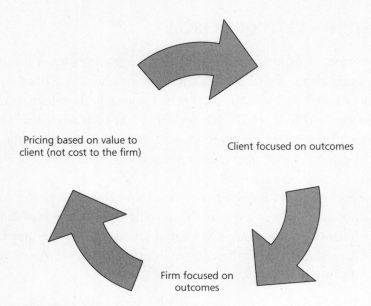

Pricing based on value to
client (not cost to the firm)

Client focused on outcomes

Firm focused on
outcomes

Figure 9.2 A Virtuous Compensation Circle

Leo Tolstoy once said, "Everyone thinks of changing the world, but no one thinks of changing himself." It won't require a commitment from the entire industry to change the pricing paradigm—just the commitment of individual firms, one firm at a time. Next we'll look at specific practices that will help your firm become part of this transformation.

CHAPTER 10

A New and Better Way to Price Professional Services

As discussed in Chapter 9, professional knowledge firms must come to the realization that clients are not buying their costs, but rather the value their firm creates. While there's a formula for cost-based billing (usually salary plus overhead plus desired profit), value-based pricing can take an almost endless variety of forms.

FORMS OF VALUE-BASED PRICING

To get started with this approach, there are three basic forms to consider: the straight fee, the usage fee, and the results fee.

Straight Fee

The simplest form of a value price is a straight fixed price based on the mutually agreed-upon value of an assignment. This is different from a traditional estimate of hours multiplied by the hourly rate, because the value associated with the price isn't correlated directly with time.

One of the best examples of a professional firm using a straight fixed price associated with value is the public affairs firm that brings tremendous value to an assignment by virtue of its contacts and relationships in government. Sometimes a single phone call can create the desired value for the client. It's really irrelevant that the firm invested only a few hours in the assignment. What's relevant—and valuable—is that the client's objective was accomplished.

Usage Fee

This option is best understood in the context of creative service firms. More and more, the best solution to a marketing problem is not a conventional advertising campaign, but rather some other form of branded content. Yet structurally agencies still operate as producers and distributors of "ads," even going so far as to stipulate that their work is "work for hire" that is wholly owned by the client.

Compare this with the creative service partners that agencies work with: actors, voice talent, models, musicians, and photographers. A photograph is owned by the photographer and licensed to the client. The more a photograph gets used, the higher the price to the marketer. The less it gets used, the lower the price. This correlated directly to the *value* of the image to the client.

For example, a photographer typically charges a flat fee to take a photograph, but this never comes close to the income the photographer needs to make the assignment profitable. The photographer's "session fee" is subsidized by the licensing fees for the use of the image. A similar approach could be used by agencies where the development of branded content is priced significantly lower than in the traditional "work for hire" model; the firm then makes its real money on the usage.

It's like the difference between renting and buying. You would never visit Miami and buy a car to provide transportation for the week.

The usage approach is perfectly aligned with value pricing because the more effective the branded content, the more it gets used, and the more the firm earns. The firm has a strong incentive to be effective, not just efficient, in the development of its work.

Results Fee

Unlike the straight fee, which is a fixed price, a "results fee" is a variable price. Examples of this type of approach include the "performance bonus" that sometimes is added to a traditional hourly based agreement. But of course a true results fee isn't built on top of a time-based foundation, and it has both an upside and a downside—true "skin in the game."

In the results fee approach, the firm ties its compensation directly to specific indicators. When identifying KPIs—key performance indicators—keep in mind that the health of a company is not measured exclusively by one metric any more than the health of the human body is measured exclusively by heart rate. A thorough evaluation of human health also would include blood pressure, temperature, organ functions, and a host of other critical metrics. So it is with the health of the brand. As Einstein said, make it simple, but not *too* simple.

Progressive consulting firms pursue this approach. Over 30 percent of Accenture's contracts include some type of performance measures.

Boston-based marketing communications firm Partners + Simons is an example of a successful independent firm that takes a value-based approach to its client relationships. To help identify the right outcomes, the firm has developed a comprehensive model that helps its clients think through the likely drivers of their brands' success. Many of these metrics are what we would call "leading indicators"—the best kind, because they predict success rather than just measure it. Examples include differentiation, likeability, perceived quality, price premium, advocacy, and participation.

Armed with the menu of possible indicators shown in Table 10.1, the firm is in a position to begin a new client relationship by discussing value instead of costs. They talk "scope of value" before discussing scope of work; expected outcomes before expected deliverables.

Imagine the impression this creates with a prospective client. The firm is asking important, intelligent questions. In the process, it very often discovers that the client organization has never really answered these questions,

Table 10.1   Success Indicators

Perception Metrics		Performance Metrics		Financial Metrics
Awareness	Consideration	Engagement	Loyalty	ROI
Recognition	Differentiation	Inquiries	Satisfaction	Revenue
Saliency	Relevance	Clicks	Retention	Cost savings
	Credibility	Views	Customer lifetime value	Cost-per-engagement
	Likeability	Conversions	Referrals	Cost-per-acquisition
	Perceived quality	Purchase	Advocacy	
	Purchase intent	Preference		
		Price premium		
		Participation		

but it becomes immediately apparent that the client should. In fact, some clients will come to view the process of identifying the metrics of success as one of the most valuable aspects of their relationship with the firm.

A discussion of scope of value should include such topics as:

* Business objectives
* Roles and responsibilities of the firm vs. the client
* Special client factors
* Process for reviewing and approving recommendations
* Desired outcomes
* Measures of success

A marketing firm in Atlanta, Fitzgerald + Company, goes so far as to hire a third-party consultant to conduct what it calls an "expectations audit" at the beginning of every major new client relationship. The purpose is to clearly identify the desired outcomes and expectations of both parties.

THE RIGHT CLIENTS FOR OUTCOME-BASED AGREEMENTS

As discussed previously, value-based compensation can take many forms, from simple project pricing based on perceived value to more sophisticated compensation agreements based on specific outcomes. The value-based pricing continuum therefore involves different levels of complexity.

While every client should be quoted pricing based on value instead of costs, only certain kinds of clients are right for the more sophisticated forms of value-based compensation involving measured outcomes.

In evaluating the potential of your clients as candidates for an outcome-based compensation agreement, here are some key factors to consider:

Do you have a high trust level with this client? Does the client seem to value what you do and treat your team with respect? Is it willing to share what often is considered to be confidential information with you? Will the client be as transparent with you as it expects you to be with it?

Is this client willing to focus time and attention on a serious project that transcends the demands of the day? Does it have the patience for a process that will take some large chunks of time, but pay rich dividends in the long term?

Is this client willing to invest in its own success? Identifying and measuring the metrics of success that will serve as the basis of an outcome-based relationship will cost money the client hasn't spent before. Is it willing to create a new line item on its budget labeled "accountability"?

The process of developing an outcome-based relationship can be intensive but extremely rewarding for both parties. Here are just a few of the benefits you can expect:

Crystal clear expectations. Once an outcome-based agreement is established, there will be no guessing or second-guessing about what the firm is expected to accomplish, and what the client is expected to do in return.

More leverage for the firm. With skin in the game and a mission to achieve specific outcomes, your firm is in a position to be much more direct and forceful in its recommendations to the client. The client is much more likely to view the firm as a partner in the true sense of the word.

The right incentive to do the right thing. Knowing what specific results need to be created, the firm is likely to be much more proactive and resourceful in how it approaches its work. Rather than worrying about how much time got logged to the client's business, the team will instead be worrying about whether they're accomplishing the outcomes.

Alignment of interests. Because the firm's compensation is tied to value created rather than hours worked, the economic interests of the firm and the client are the same. This has the potential to fundamentally change the way the client works with the firm. Instead of just barking out orders and requests, clients are much more inclined to ask, "What do you think?"

THE TRUE MEANING OF PARTNERSHIP

Survey the promotional literature of professional knowledge firms and you'll find that most of them contain the word "partnership." As if it were a unique point of difference of some kind, firms of all kinds use "partnership" as a selling point, with language like:

"We are true partners with our clients."

"We enter into every relationship as partners with our clients."

"Partnership is the very essence of the way we do business."

A national survey conducted by Ignition Consulting Group on behalf of the Association of National Advertisers and American Association of Advertising Agencies showed that most advertising firm professionals actually feel that "partnership" is missing in their client relationships. They made comments like:

"Clients need to consider the firm as part of the team, not as a vendor who can be replaced by tomorrow morning."

"Clients should stop holding power and treating agencies like ad factories."

"Agencies should be treated as a respected business partner versus the low-cost vendor."

Why the frustration among agencies? Because clients feel that most firm–client relationships don't really qualify as true partnerships. That's because the nature of a partnership is *shared risks and shared rewards*. Agencies sometimes may share in the rewards of a client's success—such as in the case of a performance bonus—but seldom do they share in the risks.

As long as agencies are compensated as vendors, they likely will be regarded as vendors. The truth is, many agencies in fact are paid like regulated utilities, with clients telling them exactly how much they can earn and what their maximum profit margin can be. That's far from the spirit of a "marketing partnership."

In partnerships, there must be both an upside and a downside to both parties—in other words, skin in the game. If you're a partner in a business, there is always both risk and reward.

Self-Confidence and Self-Worth

If professional knowledge firms are serious about becoming partners with their clients, they must stop being so risk-averse and start having more confidence the in the power of their work. When a firm is willing to tie its compensation to the same metrics that CMOs and CEOs are judged by, then it is entering into a real partnership.

More important, having skin in the game can profoundly change the dynamics of firm–client relationships, leading to increased trust and mutual respect. That's because you have aligned the economic interests of both parties. In other words, you have a partnership.

UNCOVERING MISSED OPPORTUNITIES TO MAKE PRICING A CORE COMPETENCY

To uncover the opportunities you may be missing to make pricing a pro-active competency rather than a reactive process, gather your senior executives together and review these questions:

- What's holding us back from discussing scope of value before scope of work?

- How can we do a better job of scope management by identifying and repricing work that's out of scope?

- What are the possible holes and gaps in our pricing and billing system where we might be undercharging or not charging at all for services and value delivered? Do we have a bullet-proof system of checks and balances to make sure this doesn't happen?

- What capabilities and tools do we need to put in place to help us better determine and measure value? Besides reducing or eliminating our reliance on timesheets, what else do we need to do to track and emphasize effectiveness instead of efficiency?
- What changes in process and procedures do we need to make in order to centralize pricing decisions at the firm?
- What opportunities could we pursue to develop or package our intellectual property for sale or license?
- What missed opportunities have we had to apply some creativity to pricing (rather than just estimating our costs)?
- Which of our clients would be willing to pay us more money if we take more risk?
- Could we propose a "value audit" for current or prospective clients to help identify drivers of success upon which we could base a compensation agreement?
- Would we make more money if we raised our prices on "high-value" services and lowered our prices on "low-value" services?
- Could we add value to particular services and charge more than other firms?
- Which are our low-value, unprofitable clients and what do we need to do to develop new compensation agreements with them?

KEY QUESTIONS IN SETTING A VALUE-BASED PRICE

Pricing an assignment must take into consideration many more factors than just cost (otherwise you will be doing only cost-led pricing instead of price-led costing). Here are key questions to help you both determine and validate a price based on *value delivered* instead of just costs incurred:

1. **Allocated budget**

    What is the client's budget range for this assignment? What has it allocated historically for this kind of work?

2. **Resource requirements**

   What resources (human, financial, and other) will be required to complete this assignment? Similarly, what resources will be devoted by the client?

3. **Level of talent**

   What level of talent will be needed? Does it call for our most experienced people?

4. **Degree of client involvement**

   If a client organization is willing to put an above-average amount of effort into communicating and collaborating with the firm, this should be reflected in the price. For example, many technology-savvy marketing firms have developed client extranets where clients can view work, track the status of a job, look up an invoice, or find a logo. If the client will commit to use an extranet instead of always picking up the phone or firing off an email to the account executive, it impacts the firm's investment of time and effort. The same is true with digital asset management systems and third-party project management systems, all of which improve workflow management.

5. **Scope management**

   How difficult will this assignment be to manage? Do we anticipate relatively simple project management, or is this more complex in scope?

6. **Time sensitivity**

   Is this a rush assignment that will not only disrupt our workflow, but require late nights or weekends?

7. **Financial impact**

   If this assignment succeeds in achieving its objectives, what will be the likely financial impact for the client? Conversely, what is the client's cost of *not* solving this problem?

8. **Strategic importance**

   How important is this assignment in context of the client's overall strategic objectives?

9. **Long-term value**

   In the client's value chain, are we playing a high-value, moderate-value, or low-value role? Does this assignment help create long-term value for the client, or is it essential tactical and short term?

10. **Ownership of intellectual property**

    While the whole question of IP ownership is new territory for most firms, it has a potentially significant impact on pricing. Simply put, if the client owns the IP, then the firm's value-based price should be higher than if the firm owns the IP (and therefore has the opportunity to license it back to the client).

11. **Degree of risk**

    The more risk the firm is willing to take by tying a portion of its compensation to specific outcomes, the higher the price to the client. The greater the risk, the greater the potential reward.

12. **Unique qualifications**

    Is our firm uniquely qualified to perform this work, or could it be done just as easily by someone else?

IF COMPLEX GLOBAL COMPANIES CAN DO IT, SO CAN YOU

When the world's most well-known brand, Coca-Cola, and the world's largest marketer, Procter & Gamble, adopt a value-based approach to compensating their advertising agencies, it certainly takes away one of the primary excuses of many firms: "I'll do it when I see one of the major corporations do it."

In fact, having P&G and Coke as practitioners of value-based compensation deflates a whole list of excuses:

- "I can see how value-based compensation would work for smaller organizations, but we're a big company."
- "Value-based compensation probably could work if you have a single agency relationship, but not if you have to manage multiple agencies."
- "Value-based compensation would never work for our brand; we're a global company and it would be much too complex to administer."

Coca-Cola's approach to value-based compensation is an impressive effort to align the economic incentives of its agencies with those of the Coca-Cola Company. In professional pricing circles there is a concern that the agencies (the sellers) should be setting the price instead of the client (the buyer), but Coke took this step forward because its agencies didn't.

Their new value-based approach is based on the realization that Coca-Cola is buying talent and outcomes, not structure and activities. Rather than pricing an assignment based on costs, Coke uses a five-dimensional system to evaluate value:

1. **Budget reality**. This is always a logical place to start, and historical budgets are often a good indicator of value.
2. **Scope management**. Is this project a "straight path" or will it require complex project management?
3. **Strategic priority**. The more strategically important this is to Coke, the more value.
4. **Talent**. Specific quality firm talent is always more valuable.
5. **Industry dynamics**. Is this firm uniquely qualified to do this work, or are there a lot of agencies who could do it? Unique qualifications are more valuable.[1]

Success ultimately is judged by a set of metrics established at the beginning of an assignment. Metrics can be in all or just some of the following four areas:

- Agency evaluation rating
- Specialist metrics
- Marketing communications metrics
- Business performance metrics

In the end, the real impact of Coke's new approach is that it helps shift the firm's compensation paradigm because it:

- Acknowledges that there is no correlation between labor and value.
- Begins with a discussion of "What does success look like" rather than "How many hours will it take?"

- Fundamentally changes the basis of firm compensation from hours and activities to value and outcomes.
- Seeks to apply a set of factors other than time to determine how an assignment should be priced.
- Puts in place a set of tools and processes that allow Coca-Cola marketing people to better clarify what they're trying to accomplish—scope of value, not just scope of work.
- Gets the client out of the business of controlling and dictating the firm's profit.
- Makes the concept of hourly rates and rate cards irrelevant.
- Changes the dialogue and language away from billable time, FTEs, and cost-plus to focus instead on results and performance.

Procter & Gamble, the world's largest marketer, in fact has been practicing a form of value-based compensation for years by paying its lead agencies based on sales increases of its major brands. P&G has taken this a step further by tying firm compensation to three metrics:

How did sales improve?	50% weighting
How did business share improve?	25% weighting
How did firm performance improve?	25% weighting[2]

Agency compensation can vary by 10 percent—up or down—based on these factors. Says Procter's Rich Delcore, the principal architect of this new program, "We're interested in outcomes, not deliverables."[3]

BETTER TIME TRACKING IS NOT THE ANSWER

By some estimates, the average professional service firm spends up to 20 percent of its time and energy recording, tracking, capturing, estimating, billing, and adjusting its *time*. Imagine if you took that same time and energy and instead invested it in doing a better job of identifying and managing both the scope of value and scope of work.

Suppose you're a design firm. What if you traded the time spent in column A for time spent in column B? (See Table 10.2.)

If you turned your firm's focus to column B, would the quality of your work be better? Would the client receive better value? Would you earn better margins on each assignment, and therefore on the client as a whole? The answer to all of these questions is yes. What exactly, then, is the counterargument? Why should we stay trapped in a model that serves neither party well?

Even among executives who are inclined to make the transformation from cost-based to value-based compensation, there is still a strong tendency to want to keep timesheets as a means of performing a back-end evaluation of employee performance. The argument is that without timesheets, how do you know who is an effective employee and who isn't, which department is contributing and which isn't, and who is pulling his or her weight and who isn't. The real question is: How do you know it now?

As the creators of Best Buy's successful Results Only Work Environment ask: "Do you have a mechanism in place for determining if the daily work that's being done is driving actual results, or is it assumed that if everyone is there working hard then we must be getting it right? Don't you personally know someone who isn't pulling their weight or who gets credit where credit isn't due?"[4]

Table 10.2 Trading Column A for Column B

A	B
Asking team members for estimated hours	Identifying scope of value (expected outcomes)
Preparing an estimate of hours	Clarifying scope of work
Logging hours on timesheets	Collecting complete background information
Collecting and policing timesheets	Developing more complete briefs
Tracking actual hours spent	Conducting better briefings
Inputting time in the software system	Previewing the direction with the client
Producing timesheet reports	Investing more effort in presenting the work
Reviewing time reports	Pricing (not estimating) the assignment
Reconciling actual hours against estimated hours	Pricing and billing the work in phases
Justifying hours to the client	Paying more attention to scope creep
Transferring or writing off hours	Repricing work that exceeds scope

Next time you find yourself vigorously defending the value of timesheets, ask yourself: Should your people be judged or rewarded based on time spent or results accomplished?

A Test: Life Without Timesheets

A firm in New England made the leap from cost to value by trashing timesheets, forming a Value Council, and proposing a value-based approach to all prospective clients. [5]

When the firm made the decision that timesheets serve an outdated paradigm, they shared these observations with their staff:

WHAT WE'RE GIVING UP

- Tracking utilization
- Analysis on a micro level

WHAT WE'RE GAINING

- Reduced stress between brand management and creative
- No more shell game with time
- No surprises to the client
- Fewer billing challenges
- More talk about profitability and less talk about time
- Fewer reports
- 100 percent focus on the work
- Higher profitability because value has more worth than time
- New internal language and culture
- Pricing expertise

When it comes to new business, instead of publishing a traditional schedule of hourly rates, this firm uses language like the following:

Unlike other firms, we don't sell time; we sell intellectual capital and business results. In fact, we believe that the way most firms charge work against the best interest of both the firm and the client. Hours and timesheets are focused on efficiency, and we don't believe you're buying efficiency. You're buying value, effectiveness, and results.

Because we don't bill by the hour, we don't have hourly rates. In fact, we don't even have timesheets, because timesheets only serve to point us in the wrong direction. We trade the time that would have been spent tracking internal costs and invest it in tracking the external results we create for your company.

THINKING OF COMPENSATION PLANS AS A STOCK PORTFOLIO

When creating an investment portfolio, no reasonable person would put all his or her money in just gold, just certificates of deposit, or just stocks. Now, consider the asset you have in your firm in the form of compensation agreements. If they are all based on the same approach—just fees based on hours, for example—it means you're not diversifying your portfolio.

A healthy financial portfolio includes a mixture of high risk/high return and low risk/low return. Your client compensation agreements can be viewed in much the same way. Professional financial portfolio managers are trained to optimize returns through a combination of different types and classes of investments. A professional knowledge firm can do the same with different types and classes of client compensation agreements.

Let's look at an advertising firm as an example (see Table 10.3). A firm that engages in creative compensation would have a very different "compensation portfolio" from standard agencies. Look at the risk profile of these two approaches:

Agency A undoubtedly will be operating under the illusion that if it "manages its hours" it will achieve its target profit of 15–20 percent on each client. Agency B, however, can expect much more variety in its margins, with the potential to achieve much more than the industry standard. Experience shows that the innovative firms that take this approach is that they achieve much higher profit margins, sometimes in the 30–40 percent range. Not on every client, of course, but on enough clients in their portfolio to earn the firm above-average returns.

The reaction of many firms to this line of thinking is, "This is all well and good in theory, but in the real world . . ." This implies that the firms that have made the switch to value-based compensation are not in the real world, but perhaps on another planet like Mars.

Recently a professional knowledge firm in Knoxville, Tennessee, made the transformation to a value-based approach. Upon learning about this, other firms were heard to say:

> Knoxville is a small market and our firm is in a larger market where this would not work. Or, Knoxville is a big market and our firm is in a small, tight-knit market where this would not work. Or, I can see how they could do it for current customers, but our new customers expect to be billed by the hour. Or, I can see how they could do it for new customers, but our current customers expect to be billed by the hour. Or, they are a smaller, more nimble company than we are, so this would not work for us. Or, they are a larger company with more resources than we have, so this would not work for us. And so on.[6]

Table 10.3   A Portfolio Approach to Compensation

	AGENCY A Single-Approach Compensation Portfolio	AGENCY B Diversified Compensation Portfolio
Client 1 – Luxury automobile brand	Fees based on hourly rates	$50 per car sold
Client 2 – Mobile phone accessory brand	Fees based on hourly rates	Royalty on each unit sold
Client 3 – Retail brand	Fees based on hourly rates	Value-based fixed price
Client 4 – Cosmetics brand	Fees based on hourly rates	Licensing fees for use of "webisode" series created and owned by firm
Client 5 – Financial services brand	Fees based on hourly rates	Outcome-based fee determined by achievement of specific metrics of success

You get the point. The only way out of the compensation dilemma is *through*. And the only question for your firm is *when*.

HOW WELL IS YOUR FIRM CAPTURING VALUE?

If you'd like to get a quick snapshot of where your firm is in the evolution toward a value-based business approach, ask everyone in your firm to participate in a brief ten-question survey.

Rate each question on a scale of 1 to 10, where 1 means "strongly disagree" and 10 means "strongly agree."

1. We begin every new client relationship with a discussion of Scope of Value before we discuss Scope of Work.

2. We carefully define the metrics of success at the beginning of a client relationship or major client assignment.

3. We base our relationships on how clients define success, not how we define it.

4. We have an approach that identifies the client's leading indicators of success.

5. We have the capability to develop a performance scorecard that can be used as the basis for a value-based compensation agreement.

6. In discussions with clients about pricing and compensation, we focus the dialogue around outcomes instead of efforts.

7. We apply as much creativity to client compensation as we do to solving our clients' business problems.

8. We trade the time we otherwise would spend reviewing, modifying, explaining, and defending our fees and invest it up front in defining what constitutes value in the first place.

9. We are a stakeholder in our clients' success by sharing in both the risks and the rewards.

10. We are compensated for the value of outputs instead of the cost of inputs.

You'll obviously want to look at the ratings for each individual question, but you also should calculate the overall aggregate score. If your firm scored an average of 7.0 or above, you can consider yourselves among the top-rated, value-based professional knowledge firms.

SETTING THE STAGE FOR A VALUE-BASED APPROACH TO COMPENSATION

Value-based compensation won't become the industry norm overnight. But you never know when an opportunity might present itself. It could be with the next new business prospect.

Following are some thoughts on how your firm can prepare to exploit, and even create, value-based compensation opportunities.

Appoint a Chief Value Officer

As discussed in the previous chapter, there should be one individual in the firm appointed to be the thought leader and champion of value. This is the "go to" person who understands the theory, knows the success stories, tracks developing industry practices, and leads the firm's efforts to implement the value pricing concept. This is not a task for junior or mid-management people. Ideally, the task should be given to a member of the firm's leadership group.

Start the Internal Dialogue

Make value-based compensation a key agenda item at the next meeting of your leadership team. Have your Chief Value Officer present the principles and practices and review examples of how some firms are benefiting from value-based approaches. Then have a full debate on the pros and cons, the obstacles and opportunities, to implementing value-based compensation in the firm. Expect resistance. Moving from cost-based to value-based compensation is a major change, and organizations, even creative ones like marketing firms, are not quick to embrace the change. But change will come and the winning firms will be in the vanguard.

Extend the dialogue to the full senior management team, the ones most likely to spot opportunities for value-based compensation. Demonstrate the firm's seriousness by putting a stake in the ground—say, an objective of implementing two value-based agreements with new or existing clients in the next eighteen months.

Understand How Your Clients Define Value

This is not as obvious as it seems. Not all clients define value the same way. Give each person who is responsible for senior client contact the task of meeting with his or her counterparts for the specific purpose of reviewing how the client believes the firm currently adds value and how they think it can add more value in the future. Position the meeting as part of an overall "value audit" that the firm is conducting.

Another approach is to create a "value survey" and ask key client decision makers to go online and complete a brief questionnaire. Not only will this generate useful information, but it will enhance the firm's image as a value-creating partner.

Identify Likely Value-Based Compensation Prospects

Understanding how your clients define value is the first step to determining which are the most likely prospects for a value-based agreement. But the analysis needs to go further. Here are some factors to consider:

Client trust and respect: A high degree of trust and respect for the firm at the C-level is a necessary prerequisite for a value-based agreement.

Senior client involvement: The amount of senior client involvement in providing direction or approving recommendations is indicative of how important the firm's activities are to the success of the company.

Entrepreneurial spirit: Clients with entrepreneurial management teams are more likely to see the merits in value-based agreements. Those with more bureaucratic managements will be more resistant to change and will prefer the "control" that a cost-based approach provides. They will fail to see the major risk inherent in cost-based approaches—the risk that they will receive little if any value for the fee paid.

Special situations: "Start-ups" or companies in "turnaround" mode are excellent candidates for a value-based approach.

The above is not an exhaustive list but it's a good start to creating a system to identify which clients or new business prospects are the best candidates for beginning to experiment with a value-based approach.

Prepare Hypothetical Scopes of Value

Once you've identified a couple of likely clients or prospects, have the firm's management team participate in an illuminating exercise—draw up a hypothetical scope of value (SOV) for each of them. That is, if you had free rein, what additional value could you actually create for this client? Precisely how would you do it? What would the success metrics be? What would the financial metrics of this value be to the client? Would that be sufficient to interest the client in a value-based agreement?

Then calculate what resources you would need to employ to create this value. What obstacles would you need to overcome? What changes to current work practices would need to be agreed to? Given the financial value it is receiving, what should a client be willing to pay for this value? What's the minimum price you would accept for creating this value? Congratulations—you've just laid the groundwork for a value-based compensation agreement with each of these clients. The next step is to start the dialogue with them.

Ten Ways to Negotiate Profitable Compensation

The first step in improving compensation is to commit to making pricing a core competence of your firm.

Here are some of the key principles employed by pricing professionals:

1. **Stay focused on the truth that clients are not buying your costs; they're buying outcomes, value, and utility**. Help your team understand that there is no relationship between cost and value. Your cost should not become your price. Stop estimating and start pricing. Stop negotiating cost and start negotiating value.

2. **Use the language of utility and value in place of the language of costs**. Construct RPF responses and new business presentations in a way that showcases benefits, outcomes, utility, value, and outputs rather than features, hours, inputs, activities, and efforts.

3. **Approach every compensation dialogue with this question: How can we align our economic incentives?** Make it clear you don't view

compensation as a zero-sum game. Instead of fighting with your client for a bigger slice of the pie, find ways to grow the pie.

4. **Signal to your client early in the process that you're willing to walk away**. You'll never have any leverage in a negotiation if the client believes that you'll do anything to get the business. It's counterintuitive, but wanting clients less makes them want you more.

5. **Insist on transparency of expectations in place of transparency of costs**. Show how it's in the client's best interest to discuss expected outcomes instead of expected costs. Costs are the seller's concern, not the buyer's. (Do you know what it cost to build your iPhone?)

6. **Match their process with your process**. Early in your discussions, introduce the fact that you also have a process: scope of value before scope of work.

7. **Use the principle of anchoring to get a better price**. The first figure named in a negotiation has the effect of shifting the other side's expectations of what it will have to pay. In a very real sense, the more you ask for, the more you get. Above all, stop practicing reserve-anchoring, which results from raising the possibility of discounted rates and actually lowers price expectations.

8. **Package your services and solutions in a way that makes them difficult to compare**. Remember that there is margin in mystery. By offering services or expertise not found at other firms, you can command premium pricing. Make your margins on the high-value services you provide—things that clients can't do for themselves. Stop trying to earn profits on the commoditized side of your business. Keep in mind that the buyer's job is to level the playing field. Your job is to make your service offering incomparable.

9. **In new business, extend your creative thinking to include compensation**. There are countless ways to construct compensation agreements. Falling back to cost-plus is not only ineffective; it's incredibly unimaginative for a professional advisor.

10. **Never lower price without also stripping out value; it destroys your pricing integrity**. If you reduce the price, you also must strip out value. Remember that buyers always seek to reduce price, but not necessarily value. If you're tempted to discount, keep in mind that the only winner in a price war is the buyer.

A DECLARATION OF VALUE

If you accept and practice the principles of value-based compensation, commit your firm to the following Declaration of Value:

1. We will begin each new assignment or relationship with a discussion of scope of value before we discuss scope of work.
2. We will price our services based on the value we provide rather than the hours we work.
3. We will stop estimating and start pricing.
4. We will abandon our "standard rate card" and start charging different prices to different clients at different times.
5. We will charge more for high-value services and less for low-value services, regardless of the time or cost.
6. We will commit to devote the same level of creativity to pricing and compensation as we do to solving our clients' marketing problems.
7. We will never lower price without also subtracting value.
8. We will show enough confidence to accept some risk in our compensation arrangements.
9. We will view each new client relationship as an opportunity to experiment with (and learn from) value pricing.
10. We will never enter into a pricing discussion that we're not willing to walk away from.

Nothing can change the dynamics in a client relationship more than moving away from a cost-based compensation system to one that is based on value. It gives the firm the incentive to think and be more proactive. It helps focus and prioritize the time, energies, and activities of both parties. It infuses the relationship with a higher level of trust and mutual respect, because the firm and the client are both trying to achieve the same outcomes, with the same level of risk and reward.

It's not an easy thing to do, but it's the right thing to do. The firms that show the initiative and make the move to value-based compensation will become highly attractive to a client community that is under increasing pressure to show a return on investment in professional services.

It's time for professional knowledge firms not just to work on behalf of brands, but to invest the intellectual and financial capital required to become strong brands of their own. A well-known merger and acquisitions expert working in professional services once remarked, "Show me a firm's balance sheet and I can tell you what they're worth." Can you imagine applying that kind of approach to valuing the Coca-Cola Company, Apple, or Nike? Of course not. The real value of these brands is not on their balance sheets, but in their reputations. Not just what they own, but what they stand for.

Reputational capital, by itself, does not make your firm a brand. Because most firms have yet to do the hard work of defining their brand boundaries, they are what could be considered "recognized trademarks." The opportunity—indeed the imperative—for leaders of professional knowledge firms is to not only create value for their clients, but build the value of their own firms by defining and executing a relevant, differentiated positioning strategy. In other words, professional knowledge firms need to model the behavior they preach to their clients.

The Before-and-After Survey

One way to gauge your success in defining and executing a differentiating positioning strategy is to perform a before-and-after online survey among all associates of your firm, using the questions in this appendix. Collect the data from the first survey before you begin your positioning work; this will serve as a baseline against which you can measure your progress in subsequent years. Rated questions are on a scale of 1 to 10 with 1 meaning "strongly disagree" and 10 meaning "strongly agree."

RATED QUESTIONS

- We have defined a clear focus and positioning strategy.
- We have the functions and capabilities we need to successfully deliver our value proposition.
- We have developed proprietary approaches and other intellectual capital that add value to our brand.
- We have the information resources we need to learn about and support our value proposition.
- We outsource everything that falls outside our competencies.

- We capture and share what we know about our area of expertise.
- We provide an effective means of measuring success and demonstrating accountability to our clients.
- Our people have the right skill set to support our positioning strategy.
- We use internal communication vehicles and meetings to ensure that the entire firm understands how we want to develop our brand.
- Our people understand our positioning and what they can do to help execute it in the marketplace.
- We have identified clear hiring standards for the kind of people we need in order to support our value proposition.
- We use performance reviews as a means of engaging every associate in bringing our positioning to life.
- We make sure new employees understand our positioning and business strategy.
- Our people are engaged in an ongoing professional development program that supports the goals of our desired brand.
- We have a handbook or other internal materials that explain what our value proposition is about.
- Our corporate identity reflects our positioning.
- We have a clear set of criteria for identifying prospective clients based on our positioning.
- We stand out in new business presentations by making the most of our points of difference.
- Our website reflects both the style and substance of our desired brand.
- We do an excellent job of marketing our brand and communicating the benefits of our positioning strategy to important audiences.
- Our promotional materials effectively present and differentiate our brand.
- We employ unique systems and procedures as yet another opportunity to differentiate our firm.

- We use value-based pricing as yet another opportunity to differentiate our agency.
- We take steps to develop and own our own intellectual property.
- Our positioning is reflected in the way we create first impressions: our email, voice mail, phone answering, and so forth.
- Our offices reflect our positioning.
- We use technology to help us create a competitive point of difference.

OPEN-ENDED QUESTIONS

- How do you feel about how the new positioning is unfolding?
- Compared with a year ago, what are the most positive changes you see in our firm?
- What are your thoughts about how we can remove obstacles to success and do an even better job of developing and aligning our brand in the future?

TRACKING YOUR SUCCESS

Many firms are in the habit of conducting this type of internal survey every year and sharing the results with associates as a means of keeping everyone informed and engaged in the firm's future success. In this way, you can ensure that you are staying true to your positioning strategy by continuing to defend and support a relevant, differentiating value proposition that will serve your firm for years to come.

More Ways to Differentiate Your Brand

Chapter 8 presented the five S's for differentiating your firm's brand, including Services, Staffing, Self-promotion, Systems, and Staging. Here you'll find even *more* ways to make your brand stand out and succeed.

SERVICES

- Proposal development
- Strategic planning approach
- New product/service development approach
- Competitive information collection approach
- Secondary research approach
- Primary research approach
- New client start-up program
- Client metrics measurement system
- Client relationship evaluation program
- Client review process

STAFFING

- Employment agreements
- Employee compensation approach
- Titles
- Job and role descriptions
- Employee benefits
- Employee termination policy and procedures
- Information sharing
- Talent management system
- Availability and use of administrative help

SELF-PROMOTION

- Business development research
- New business inquiry handling
- Speaking program
- Approach to RFP and questionnaire development
- Presentation style and approach
- Publications and white papers
- Custom research studies
- Webinars and events
- Approach to case study development

SYSTEMS

- Resource scheduling
- Work hours
- Billing approach
- Past-due collection approach
- Approach to meetings, including online meetings

- Separating the production of work from the production of intellectual capital
- Profit-sharing approach

STAGING

- Internal intranets
- Client extranets
- Dress code
- Email and mobile phone usage and policies
- Nameplates
- Signage
- Restrooms
- Conference and meeting rooms
- Meeting room accessories
- Catering supplies
- Computer desktops and laptop lids

Indicators of the Firm's Success

D o you know what predicts your firm's success? Most success metrics measure only what *has* happened, using what could be called "lagging indicators." But imagine the effectiveness of your brand development efforts if you could identify the "leading indicators" for your firm: the activities, customer behaviors, and measurements that actually lead to revenues and profits.

Instead of just looking in the rear view mirror at historical measurements like revenues, leading indicators look ahead; they're focused on the actual precursors of business success. Most leading indicators never appear on a financial statement, but they can—and should—be identified and tracked.

Leading Indicators	Lagging Indicators
Predictive	Diagnostic
Forward-looking	Backward-looking
Attitudinal and behavioral	Transactional
A measurement tied to a hypothesis	A measurement

Identifying the real causes of your firm's health is vital to implementing a successful change in business strategy. To cite an example from the consumer world, most brands with call centers commonly measure such things as time on hold and minutes per call. But these metrics don't measure or predict real customer satisfaction; they are only lagging indicators. Research by Convergys shows that customer satisfaction is predicted by two things:

1. Is the customer service representative knowledgeable?
2. Is the problem resolved on the first call?

By working to improve the leading indicators, you necessarily will improve the lagging indicators.[1]

While predictive is better than historical, this isn't to say there isn't a place for lagging indicators in measuring the success of your efforts. Naturally you'll want to track things like growth in revenues and profits.

But beware; many traditional measures of success are the result of historical practices rather than a careful study of cause and effect. Correlation is not the same thing as causation. As Einstein said, "Not everything that counts can be counted, and not everything that can be counted counts."

While specific success indicators certainly will vary based on your industry, here are some good candidates to consider.

EXAMPLES OF LAGGING INDICATORS

Lagging indicators are simply measurements that involve objective calculations such as:

- Total revenues
- Salaries as a percent of gross revenues
- Revenue per employee
- Total operating profit
- Profit as a percent of gross income
- Profitability of your top ten clients
- Growth in gross income

- Year-over-year increase in income from current clients
- Overhead as a percent of direct expenses
- Working capital as a percent of average monthly operating expenses
- Current ratio (current assets/current liabilities)
- Client turnover ratio
- Employee turnover ratio
- Percent of assignments and engagements completed on time
- Days from close of month to final billing
- Average aging for accounts receivable

EXAMPLES OF LEADING INDICATORS

Leading indicators help predict—rather than measure—your success. For professional knowledge firms, these could include such indicators as:

- Percent of assignments or engagements with clearly identified scope
- Percent of top clients for which a quarterly "scope audit" is conducted
- Percent of clients resigned due to lack of profitability or potential
- Percent of new associates oriented about the firm's positioning strategy
- Hours of professional development per employee
- Percent of performance plans completed
- Number of staff or management meetings held
- Number of speeches to business organizations
- Number of articles or white papers published
- Number of prospects declined due to strategic fit
- Percent of assignments or engagements proactively priced vs. billed by the hour
- Percent of assignments or engagements repriced due to scope creep
- Income derived from changes in scope
- Percent of associates fluent in the use of the firm's major software systems
- Income from the sale or licensing of intellectual property

Leading indicators can also be in the form of subjective ratings, as determined by the senior executives of the firm. Following are some examples organized by the five S's presented in Chapter 8.

SERVICES

- We do a good job of clarifying expectations and outcomes at the beginning of major assignments and client relationships.
- We take the lead in helping our clients plan ahead in order to get adequate time to do our best work.
- We are focused on what we do best and have found business partners for the rest.
- We invest the appropriate time and energy in staying current on our clients' business.
- We help our clients do annual planning.
- We help our clients identify and prioritize initiatives that have the greatest potential.
- We have the information resources we need to be experts in our area of focus.
- We have developed a body of intellectual capital that supports our positioning and adds value to clients.
- We effectively orchestrate and integrate functions, departments, and services.
- We regularly develop and deliver proactive thinking and ideas.
- We emphasize the services that provide the highest value to our clients.
- We are persuasive and effective in presenting and defending our work and recommendations.
- We have a system for measuring our clients' success and showing accountability for results.
- We catalogue what we learn in a knowledge base available to all associates.
- We are effective at growing current client business.

STAFFING

- We have a well-defined organizational structure.
- We have clearly defined the roles and responsibilities of every associate.
- We assign our best talent to our best clients and our best opportunities.
- We have a performance planning and review system that clearly articulates expected outcomes for every associate.
- We recognize and reward exceptional performance.
- We have an established management team that meets regularly to address key issues and initiatives.
- Our managers and supervisors provide regular feedback and coaching.
- We regularly solicit input and feedback from all associates.
- We communicate news and information regularly and keep members of the firm well informed.
- We have a rigorous professional development program.
- We train our supervisors and department heads in the art of management.
- We thoroughly orient and indoctrinate all new associates.
- We have a mentoring program for new employees.
- We have clear hiring standards for the kind of people we need in order to deliver on our business strategy.
- We have an employee handbook that helps associates understand both agency policies and culture.
- We have tools, in addition to just interviews and resumes, for evaluating the best potential employees.
- Everyone is aware of the firm's goals and how they are expected to contribute.
- Associates are compensated fairly, given the size of the firm and the market.
- The leaders of the firm have an effective and productive working relationship.

- Associates have an opportunity to grow and advance in the firm.
- We have identified a career path for our best people.
- Our people feel vested in the success of the firm.
- Leadership of the firm is committed to move the company forward in new and innovative ways.
- We put a premium on finding and hiring the very best talent.

SELF-PROMOTION

- We have an up-to-date and consistently executed corporate identity (including online forms and formats).
- Our new business approach and materials focus on our positioning—our point of relevant differentiation.
- We have well-defined criteria—both objective and subjective—for identifying and selecting prospective clients.
- We engage in inventive and unorthodox forms of promotion for our own brand.
- We actively avoid using the typical language other firms in our industry use to describe themselves.
- Our website is an effective virtual representation of our firm.
- We have a program to actively monitor and build our online reputation.
- We demonstrate our knowledge and expertise by speaking, writing, and publishing.
- We market our brand to all important audiences, not just prospective clients.
- We stand out in new business presentations by making the most of our point of difference.

SYSTEMS

- We proactively manage workload based on capacity rather than arbitrary client demands.
- We have effective project management systems and procedures.

- We develop work that's right the first time and avoid numerous rounds of revisions.
- Our organization follows the practice of pricing based on value vs. estimating based on costs.
- We have made pricing a core competency in our firm by teaching it to front-line associates.
- We have identified the best pricers in our organization and have put them in a position of pricing authority.
- We are willing to experiment with compensation in order to continually learn how to capture more value for what we do.
- We have a good system for identifying and charging for work outside of scope.
- We routinely review and resign unprofitable, undesirable clients.
- We are attempting to own or license more and more of our intellectual property.
- We are exploring and developing new revenue centers that transcend the traditional "work for hire" model of professional service firms.
- We keep within client timetables and budgets.
- We are not dependent on timesheets to assess the value we create for our clients.

STAGING

- Our offices present a positive reflection of our brand.
- We create positive first impressions at all major points of contact with our brand (reception, voice mail, email, and so on).
- We have appropriate guidelines for furnishings and décor that help reinforce our brand image.
- We have an effective digital asset management system that is understood and used by all associates.
- We provide associates with the necessary tools and equipment they need in order to do their best work.

- We have established an appropriate amount of workspace for collaboration (vs. individual offices).
- We enable our associates to work virtually anywhere in the world.
- We have leveraged technology not only to help make us more effective, but to help create a competitive point of difference.

Knowing the metrics that matter for your firm is key to successfully executing your positioning strategy. By measuring what matters, you can make your investment of time and resources go much further.

Notes

INTRODUCTION

1. Mark Earls and Alex Bently, "Forget Influencials, Herd-Like Copying Is How Brands Spread," *Admap*, November 2008.
2. James Gregory, CEO, Core Brand, citing statistics from the consultancy's 2008 BrandPower rankings study.

CHAPTER 1: SIZE IS NOT A STRATEGY

1. Peter Walshe and Helen Fearn, "Brand Equity and the Bottom Line," *Admap*, March 2008.
2. Michael Marn, Eric Roegner, and Craig Zawadam, *The Price Advantage*, John Wiley & Sons, 2004.
3. William Poundstone, *Priceless*, Hill & Wang, 2010.
4. Richard Miniter, *The Myth of Market Share*, Crown Business, 2002.
5. From Jim Collins, *How the Mighty Fall and Why Some Companies Never Give In*, HarperCollins, 2009.
6. Bo Burlingham, *Small Giants*, Penguin Group, 2005.
7. Richard Kirshenbaum and Jonathan Bond, *Under the Radar*, John Wiley & Sons, 1998.
8. Jonah Bloom "Recession Provides a Chance to Build a Better Capitalism," *Advertising Age*, December 8, 2008.
9. Alvin Silk and Ernst Berndt, "Holding Companies: Size-Related Cost Economies," *Admap*, September 2005.
10. Larry Ribstein, "The Death of Big Law," Illinois Law and Economics Research Paper Series, 2009.

CHAPTER 2: HOW AND WHY BRANDS BECOME HOMOGENIZED

1. Copernicus and Greenfield study referenced in "From Share Leader to True Brand Leader," *Admap* December 2007.
2. Al Ries, *Focus*, HarperBusiness, 1996.
3. Clayton Christensen, "Meeting the Challenge of Disruptive Change" *Harvard Business Review*, December 2008.
4. Clayton M. Christensen, Scott Cook, and Taddy Hall, "Marketing Malpractice: The Cause and the Cure," *Harvard Business Review*, December 2005.
5. From www.disruption.com.
6. Al Ries, "Slowly But Surely, Line Extensions Will Take Your Brand Off Course," *Advertising Age*, September 7, 2009.

CHAPTER 3: THE MATURE COMPANY'S IDENTITY CRISIS

1. Based on the work of Clayton Christensen and Michael Raynor in *The Innovator's Solution*, Harvard Business School Press, 2003.
2. Michael Porter, *On Competition*, Harvard Business School Publishing, 1985.
3. David Baker, "Navigating an Economic Downturn," *Communication Arts*, 2008.
4. Findings from Young & Rubicam's Brand Asset Valuator as reported in Susan Bernstein, "From Share Leader to True Brand Leader," *Admap*, December 2007.
5. As described by Al Ries and Laura Ries in *War in the Boardroom*, Collins Business, 2009.
6. "Middle-Class Struggle," *The Economist*, November 28, 2009.
7. Jonas Ridderstrale and Kjell A. Nordstrom, *Karaoke Capitalism: Daring to Be Different in a Copycat World*, Praeger, 2005.

CHAPTER 4: EXPANDING YOUR BUSINESS BY NARROWING FOCUS

1. Eric Ryan, CEO, Method, quoted at the Financial Management Conference of the Association of National Advertisers, April 2009.
2. Chip Souba, "Leading Again for the First Time," *Journal of Surgical Research*, 2009.
3. "Invisible But Indispensable," *The Economist*, November 7, 2009.

4. Millward Brown Study on Agency New Business commissioned by the American Association of Advertising Agencies, 2007.
5. Andrew McMains "New Study Reveals What a Client Wants in an Agency," *Adweek*, December 15, 2009.
6. 2009 Trending Report by Mirren Business Development presented at the Mirren New Business Conference, 2009.
7. Bain/IAB Marketer Survey, 2009.
8. Rupal Parekh "QVC Hires Zimmerman for Social Media, Digital Work," *Advertising Age*, December 14, 2009.
9. "Global Swap Shops," *The Economist*, January 30, 2010.

CHAPTER 5: POSITIONING AS THE CENTERPIECE OF BUSINESS STRATEGY

1. Tarun Khanna and Jan Rivkin, "Estimating the Performance Effects of Business Groups in Emerging Markets," *Strategic Management Journal*, 2001.
2. Chris Zook with James Allen, *Profit from the Core*, Harvard Business School Press, 2001.
3. Frances X. Frei, "The Four Things a Service Business Must Get Right," *Harvard Business Review*, April 2008.
4. Theodore Levitt, *Ted Levitt on Marketing*, Harvard Business School Publishing 2006.
5. David J. Collins and Cynthia A. Montgomery. "Competing on Resources," *Harvard Business Review*, July–August 2008.
6. Peter Drucker, *The Essential Drucker*, CollinsBusiness, 2001.
7. Blog, "Creating Passionate Users," by Kathy Sierra.
8. W. Chan Kim and Renee Mauborgne, *Blue Ocean Strategy*, Harvard Business School Press, 2005.
9. Mark Ritson, "Should You Launch a Fighter Brand?" *Harvard Business Review*, October 2009.

CHAPTER 6: BUILDING BRAND BOUNDARIES

1. Michael Porter, "What Is a Strategy?" *Harvard Business Review*, 1996.
2. Peter Drucker, *The Effective Executive*, HarperBusiness, 1996.

3. Howard Gardner, "Ethical Mind: A Conversation with Psychologist Howard Gardner" Harvard Business Review, May 2007.

4. As quoted by Norman Berry, Ogilvy & Mather, in internal documents published in 1983.

5. From a presentation delivered at a conference of the Association of National Advertisers, Scottsdale, 2009.

6. Alex Bogusky of Crispin Porter + Bogusky writing on his blog, September 2009. http://alexbogusky.posterous.com/

7. Frederick Herzberg, "How Do You Motivate Employees?" *Harvard Business Review*, January–February 1968.

8. Peter Drucker, *The Practice of Management*, Harper & Row, 1982.

9. Paul Arden, "It's Not How Good You Are, It's How Good You Want To Be," Phaidon, 2003.

10. Study by Catalina Marketing and the CMO Council, as published in *Advertising Age*, December 8, 2008.

11. "Natural Born Clickers" study by ComScore and Starcom.

12. Larry Selden and Yoko Selden, "Profitable Customer: The Key to Great Brands," *Advertising Age*, July 10, 2006.

13. Jack Bergstrand, *Reinvent Your Enterprise*, The Drucker Institute. 2009.

14. Chris Anderson, *The Long Tail*, Hyperion, 2006.

15. Chris Zook, *Unstoppable*, Harvard Business School Press, 2007.

16. Gary Hamel and C.K. Prahalad, *Competing for the Future*, Harvard Business Press, 1996.

17. David Angelo, "Be Brave," *One: A Magazine*, 2008.

18. Quoted from a speech by Dan Weiden to the American Association of Advertising Agencies, New Orleans, 2008.

19. Ayn Rand, *The Fountainhead*, Penguin, 2005.

CHAPTER 7: VALIDATING YOUR VALUE PROPOSITION

1. Inspired by the work of Clayton Christenson and Michael Raynor in *The Innovator's Solution*, Harvard Business School Publishing, 2003.

2. Tom Monahan, *The Do-It-Yourself Lobotomy*, John Wiley & Sons, 2002.

3. Alex Bogusky and John Winsor, *Baked In*, Agate Publishing, 2009.

CHAPTER 8: WITHOUT EXECUTION, THERE IS NO STRATEGY

1. "Detroit's Wounded Giant," *The Economist*, November 19, 2005.
2. Larry Bossidy and Ram Charan, *Execution*, Crown Business, 2002.
3. Presentation by Heather Fullerton, partner at Strawberry Frog, Utah Advertising Federation, 2005.
4. As quoted on the PARAGRAPH Project website, www.theparagraphproject.com.
5. This model was adapted from the work of Ric Merrifield, Jack Calhoun, and Dennis Stevens as published in *Harvard Business Review*, June 2008, under the title "The Next Revolution in Productivity."
6. Lamalile Report on Top Executives of the 1990s.
7. Based on findings from the Agency Brand Assessment from Ignition Consulting Group.
8. As reported in Charlene Li and Josh Bernoff, *Groundswell*, Harvard Business Press, 2008.
9. Based on the work of Ron Baker and my colleagues at the VeraSage Institute.
10. Cali Ressler and Jody Thompson, *Why Work Sucks and How to Fix It*, Penguin Group, 2008.
11. Gary Hamel with Bill Breen, *The Future of Management*, Harvard Business School Press, 2007.
12. Joe Phelps, *Pyramids Are Tombs*, IMC Publishing, 2002.
13. Peter Drucker, *The Essential Drucker*, HarperCollins, 2001.
14. Jack Bergstrand, *Reinvent Your Enterprise*, The Drucker Institute, 2009.
15. Marilyn Baxter, "Magic and Logic," white paper prepared for the Institute of Practitioners of Advertising, 2006.
16. From Mary Walton and W. Edwards Deming, *The Deming Management Method*, Pedigree, 1988.
17. Peter Keen, *The Process Edge*, Harvard Business School Press, 1997.
18. *Creative Review*, May 2008.
19. Quoted from a presentation by Clive Wilkinson to the American Association of Advertising Agencies, New Orleans, 2008.
20. Jack Bergstrand, *Reinvent Your Enterprise*, The Drucker Institute. 2009.
21. Joann Lublin, "Keeping Clients by Keeping Workers," *Wall Street Journal*, November 20, 2006.
22. Based on the work of Peter Block in *The Answer to How Is Yes*, Berrett-Koehler, 2003.

CHAPTER 9: GETTING PAID FOR CREATING VALUE

1. As quoted in a presentation given at the AAAA Management Conference, Scottsdale, 2006.
2. Quoted from a speech by Rory Sutherland accepting his new position as president of the UK's Institute of Practitioners of Advertising.
3. Jared Spool, "The $300 Million Button," 2009, as published at www.uie.com.
4. "Billing Methods Survey," American Association of Advertising Agencies, 2007.

CHAPTER 10: A NEW AND BETTER WAY TO PRICE PROFESSIONAL SERVICES

1. From a presentation by Sarah Armstrong, Coca-Cola Company, Association of National Advertisers (ANA) Financial Management Conference, Scottsdale, April 2009.
2. As presented during the ANA Financial Management Conference, Scottsdale, April 2009.
3. As presented during the ANA Financial Management Conference, Scottsdale, Arizona, April 2009.
4. Cali Ressler and Jody Thompson, *Why Work Sucks and How to Fix It*, Penguin, 2008.
5. Based on the experience of Kelliher Samets Volk, headquartered in Burlington, Vermont, with offices in Boston and New York.
6. From a blog post by Ed Kless, 2009, www.verasage.com.

APPENDIX C: INDICATORS OF THE FIRM'S SUCCESS

1. Convergys 2008 U.S. Customer Scorecard.

Tim Williams is a veteran of the advertising and marketing business who now leads Ignition Consulting Group (www.ignitiongroup.com), a business consultancy devoted to helping professional knowledge firms create and capture more value.

As a recognized thought leader in the creative services industry, Tim is a frequent speaker and presenter for business organizations and associations worldwide. He is also a frequent contributor to business and professional publications and is author of *Take a Stand for Your Brand*, ranked at one time by Amazon as one of the top ten books on brand building. Based on his expertise in the area of building differentiated brands, Tim has been interviewed by such diverse news-gathering organizations as *The Economist, Bloomberg News, The Guardian, The Globe & Mail,* Japan's *Nikkei News,* Advertising Age, Adweek, and other business publications in countries ranging from Spain to Australia.

Tim is also a Senior Fellow of the VeraSage Institute (www.verasage .com), a think tank devoted to revolutionizing the way professional service firms price and value their services. As an advisor in this area, Tim has worked with major advertising agencies, agency holding companies, Fortune 500 marketers, and national and international trade associations.

He began his career on Madison Avenue working for large multinational advertising agencies and later served as president and CEO of several mid-sized independent firms. As the leader of Ignition Consulting Group, Tim now advises the leaders and managers of professional knowledge firms on the development and execution of positioning strategies.

The author invites you to continue to explore the concepts of this book at www.positioningforprofessionals.com and to follow @TimWilliamsICG on Twitter.

Index